THE
INSIDERS

THE
INSIDERS

The Truth Behind the Scandal
Rocking Wall Street

Mark Stevens

Researched by Carol Bloom Stevens

HARRAP London

First published in Great Britain 1987
by HARRAP Ltd
19-23 Ludgate Hill, London EC4M 7PD

First published by G.P. Putnam's Sons 1987

ISBN 0 245–54613 8

Printed and bound in Great Britain
by Mackays of Chatham Limited

To Harry

CONTENTS

I

Tip of the Iceberg

"Maybe we should rewrite the compliance warning we send to our young investment bankers, changing it from 'You'll ruin your career, blah, blah, blah,' to something more ominous like 'Engage in insider trading and we'll kill you!'"
—JIM BALOG, *vice-chairman of Drexel Burnham Lambert, on careers, compliance and insider trading*

On the evening of May 12, 1986, investment banker Dennis Levine—only hours before a prince of Wall Street—surrendered himself at the grim, gray offices of the U.S. Attorney for the Southern District of New York. Trembling and colorless, as if the blood had been drawn from his veins, Levine listened in disbelief as federal prosecutor Charles Carberry—a big Burl Ives of a man—read his Miranda rights.

"You have the right to an attorney. If you do not have an attorney . . ."

Moments later, a burly police sergeant locked handcuffs around the banker's wrists, marking the beginning of the end of the greatest insider trading scheme in U.S. history—one that would blacken Wall Street's reputation and shatter some of its most illustrious careers.

Within hours, news of Levine's arrest brought to the surface the tawdry details of a byzantine trading scheme replete with code names, secret bank accounts, a ring of accomplices, cash payoffs and unbridled greed. In roughly five years, Levine had misused his position as an investment banker with some of the Street's most prominent institutions to amass a personal fortune of $12.6 million—all squirreled away in the Nassau, Bahamas, branch of Zurich-based Bank Leu International. Before it was over, he would implicate a clique of financial overlords including the high priest of arbitrage—and the Street's most flamboyant personality—Ivan Boesky.

11

Word of Levine's scheme spread through Wall Street like rumors of an Icahn takeover, turning the young banker's name, once so bright and glittery, into an object of scorn and hatred.

"Before anyone here had a chance to speak to Dennis—before the ink was dry on his arrest warrant—the verdict was that Levine was as guilty as a Colombian drug dealer," says a client of Levine's last employer, Drexel Burnham Lambert, a hardball investment banking firm widely hated and widely imitated by its white-shoe competitors. "Guys who the day before thought Dennis walked on water were calling him scum. He'd sinned; more than that, he made it seem as if they'd all sinned—and for that he'd never be forgiven.

"But what was his sin? That he wanted to be rich—Rockefeller-rich—before he reached thirty-five? That he went to work for a firm that could make his dreams a reality? To a firm that paid him a millon dollars a year to do almost exactly what he's going to jail for? In truth, the only sin he committed is that he did what he did for his personal gain as well as for the firm's. But if you think that's unique, you know nothing about Wall Street.

"Let's make one thing clear: trading on inside information isn't some scandalous little subchapter of the investment banking business. It's the way much of the big money is made in the stock market. When you dissect the mergers and acquisitions that fuel most of the Big Board activity, you find that these deals bring together companies, yes, but more than that they bring together people. An incestuous little cast of characters who know all there is to know and who find it good business to share that information—in some cases illegally—with each other."

It has always been that way. The Levine/Boesky case simply focused attention on a problem that has been around, tainting the financial markets since the first day shares were publicly traded. As long as there have been insiders—as long as those involved in managing or advising companies have learned of corporate developments before the public—there have been insider trades.

The temptation to profit from advance information, and to do so with no more effort than calling a stockbroker and placing an order, has proven irresistible. Since 1980 alone, the U.S. Attorney's Office for the Southern District of New York has prosecuted forty-eight individuals for insider trading. Others have settled directly with the Securities and Exchange Commission (SEC), and countless more have evaded detection.

In spite of the fairy tale foisted on the public by the major stock exchanges—primarily the Big Board and the Amex—that the markets provide equal opportunity for all investors, the fact is that they are more like rigged casinos. Those who know how the system works, and who can gain access to corporate intelligence, routinely shift the odds in their favor. Once the news is out, once the public knows what the insiders have whispered about for weeks or months, the real profit has already been skimmed from the top.

Guy Wyser-Pratte, chief arbitrager for Prudential-Bache Securities and an outspoken market observer, puts it this way:

"Some people aren't playing by the rules, and that stinks. When you take risks and play by the rules, you want everyone to do the same. When they don't—and when they get away with it—there's a feeling of fair play that gets trampled upon."

That some of the players get a jump on the market is demonstrated by the remarkable chart on p. 14, which shows the sharp price gains in twelve takeover stocks (some traded by Levine and Boesky) shortly *before* their acquisitions were announced.

Chronic leaks frustrate even the takeover artists. When British-French investor Sir James Goldsmith considered acquiring the Continental Group, he first tested the ability of Wall Street's investment banking firms to keep a client's confidences. Informing three firms of fictitious takeover targets, he waited to see if the news would leak. Sure enough, one of the companies he had named quickly wound up in a syndicated newspaper column as the subject of an acquisition rumor.

In another case, Texas billionaire H. Ross Perot recalls that when he was negotiating to sell his company, Electronic Data

STOCK PRICES IN TWELVE MAJOR TAKEOVERS

Company	One month before offer ($)	One day before offer ($)	Offer price ($)	Gain in one month
ABC	66	105⅞	121	83%
American Natural Resources	42¼	53¾	65	54%
Beatrice Companies	33¼	44⅜	47	41%
General Foods	77⅛	101½	120	56%
Houston Natural Gas	46⅝	58⅝	70	50%
R. H. Macy	44	47⅛	70	59%
MGM/UA Entertainment	15¼	22⅝	29	90%
Nabisco	59½	71⅜	85	43%
Pacific Lumber	28⅞	33	40	39%
Richardson-Vicks	38½	46⅛	69	79%
G. D. Searle	53	63¾	65	23%
Stauffer Chemical	18⅜	27	28	52%
Average Gain				55.7%

Sources: Glen Parker, the Institute for Econometric Research, Fort Lauderdale, Florida; Valerie Tyler, W. T. Grimm Company, Chicago, Illinois. Reprinted by permission of Dan Dorfman, *USA Today* columnist.

Systems, to General Motors, the status of the talks would leak out time and again.

"We had a good meeting and the stock went up; we had a bad meeting and stock went down. I finally called the guys [who attended the meetings] in and I said, "Now, if this happens anymore, I'm going to find out who did it. We're going to get this straightened out because this is rotten, absolutely rotten. And interestingly enough, it stopped."

In the classic case, the inside trader is part of the corporate structure, a member of its management team or board of directors. From this vantage point he learns of, and often helps to shape, every material development in the corporation's affairs. Blessed with this foresight, this crystal ball of sorts, he invests in a string of "sure things."

"Some of the biggest inside traders are the corporate directors," says a mergers-and-acquisitions (M&A) specialist with the CPA firm of Arthur Young. "You'll find in their ranks a mini—Who's Who of the biggest, most prominent names in American business and industry.

"These guys have an old-boy network like no other. They serve together on the same boards, join the same golf clubs, sail in the same regattas. In their privileged little world, it's de rigueur to impress each other with how much they know about this or that company, this or that stock. Blue-collar guys boast about their bowling scores. Directors play a more upscale game.

"How does the trading work? The boys are lounging in the clubhouse after a long eighteen holes and director Smith lets it drop that Fly High Airlines, on whose board he sits, has taken a shine to its thorn-in-the-side competitor, Cheap Air. The message, in so many words, is that Cheap Air will soon be bought, merged into Fly High and dissolved.

"Acting on this still secret (haha) plan, those directors inclined to pocket a quick gain when they see one call their brokers for a few thousand shares of Cheap Air. Not enough to make pigs of themselves—and in the process alert the SEC—but more than enough to pay for the annual club dues. Smith, for his part, doesn't buy any. He'd be too easy to trace. Instead, he waits for the time when fellow directors Jones or Kline or O'Connor can return the favor, alerting him to a pending takeover when it is still (haha) secret."

Before Levine and Boesky grabbed the headlines, the grand shocker of insider trading schemes did indeed involve a corporate director, one Paul Thayer, who just happened to be a friend of the president of the United States.

A former naval aviator and test pilot who had once flown in a daring formation under the Golden Gate Bridge, Thayer rose to become chief executive of the Dallas-based LTV Corporation, a steel and aerospace giant. A tough administrator impatient with bureaucracy and intolerant of waste, Thayer became a popular fixture on corporate boards, serving as a director for Anheuser-Busch and Allied Corporation before accepting Ronald Reagan's nomination to become deputy secretary of defense in 1983.

He would hold the post for less than a year. In January 1984 the SEC charged Thayer with being the central figure in an insider trading ring that involved a cast of good old boys (and girls) fit for starring roles on the television show *Dallas*.

The scheme began in the summer of 1981, when LTV took a shine to Grumman Corporation, a Bethpage, New York–based aerospace contractor. Convinced that Grumman would make an attractive addition to its own business, LTV secretly explored the idea of a tender offer for Grumman's stock and, testing the waters, proceeded to shop the deal with three commercial banks (which would lend the money) and a Wall Street investment banking firm (which would act as a dealer/manager for the tender offer). As LTV's chief executive and chairman of the board, Thayer orchestrated the pretakeover jockeying.

In the midst of these behind-the-scenes negotiations, Thayer allegedly leaked word of LTV's plans to his stockbroker and close buddy Billy Bob Harris, the star salesman in the Dallas office of the A. G. Edwards brokerage firm. A handsome man-about-town who hosted his own television program and ranked in local celebrity on a par with Cowboys football coach Tom Landry, Harris was friend and broker to a star-studded roster of clients, including crooner Kenny Rogers and former Dallas Cowboy quarterback turned *Monday Night Football* color commentator Dandy Don Meredith. He thus became the only broker ever to be plugged on *Monday Night Football*. "Aw shucks," Meredith once commented on a player's fame, "back in Dallas he's known as Billy Bob Harris's roommate."

Though he was the most famous recipient of Thayer's "secret" information, the leak didn't end with Billy Bob. According to the SEC, Thayer, and in turn Harris, then passed word of the pending Grumman takeover to a circle of friends, lovers and business associates, including physician Doyle Sharp; banker Gayle Schroder; Dallas insurance agency president Malcolm Davis; and William Mathis, a longtime friend of Harris and broker with the Atlanta office of Bear Stearns.

But the end was nowhere in sight. In a chain reaction typical of insider leaks, the SEC charged that Mathis tipped off a Bear Stearns colleague, who agreed to pay him 50 percent of the profits he would earn on Grumman stock. Convinced that Mathis was on to something, the Bear Stearns rep then cut a similar deal with a New York broker, by whispering word of the Grumman stock and staking a 50-percent claim on the profits from that purchase. Davis—for years a client of Billy Bob Harris—reportedly hotlined two friends in Boston about the Grumman deal, and sought and won the same 50-percent profit-sharing stake.

The greed was contagious. "Between September 17 and 22, 1981," according to the SEC, "more than 100,000 shares of Grumman common stock were purchased by friends and associates of Harris, Mathis, Schroder and Davis, and by persons known to such friends and associates. On September 17 and 18, the purchases by such persons, combined with purchases made by Mathis, Schroder and Davis, accounted for approximately 70 percent of the total volume of trading in Grumman common stock on those two days."

Then the news they were waiting for hit the Dow Jones wire. On September 23, for the first time, LTV announced that it was launching a tender offer and bidding $45 a share for Grumman stock and convertible debentures. The market reacted accordingly, driving Grumman shares from an opening price of $26¾ to $35⅞ at the closing bell. In the weeks to follow, shares owned by the Thayer group or shares in which they had a stake were sold off, and they generated illegal profits of about $800,000. Thayer, who never conducted insider trading for his own account, did not gain financially from the transactions.

But he would see to it that his girlfriend did. Later in 1981 he became aware that LTV, which had been mired in an earnings slump, would demonstrate a dramatic turnaround and report sharply higher profits for the year. Knowing that LTV's audit committee was scheduled to meet on January 27, 1982, to prepare a press release announcing the fiscal recovery—and that the finance committee would convene the following day to consider reinstituting LTV's cash dividend—Thayer allegedly lateraled this "secret" information to his girlfriend, former LTV receptionist Sandra Ryno, and to Billy Bob Harris.

Blessed with the scoop from the boss, Harris purchased LTV stock through margin accounts maintained with him at A. G. Edwards. One purchase was for 8,500 shares at $14 each; another 1,500 shares were bought at prices between $13⅞ and $14. Both orders were issued before 11:00 A.M. Eastern time on January 27.

Less than an hour later, after the audit committee had met, the Dow Jones news wire carried a report that LTV's earnings had more than tripled, soaring from $127.9 million in 1980 to $386.3 million in 1981. Reacting to the bullish news, the market pushed up LTV's stock by almost 2 points.

But the best was yet to come. On January 27—after LTV issued its earnings release—Harris, according to the SEC, gobbled up 10,000 of the corporation's shares for his own account and on January 28 took another 10,000 shares for his father's account and an additional 13,000 shares to be split among three of his customers.

As this buying spree was progressing, LTV's finance committee, in a meeting attended by Thayer, decided to recommend that the board of directors reinstitute the dividend. The next day, the board met on the issue and voted in favor of a 12.5-cent dividend per share. Within hours, word was issued to the press and, in turn, to the investment community.

It was time to cash in the chips. On February 1, the first day of trading after the dividend notice, two of Thayer's friends liquidated their shares, taking profits of $16,930 and $2,713. Harris—who had pledged his shares to secure a bank loan—could not sell until April, but his father's account showed profits of more than $7,000. Once again, the Thayer connection proved to be a sure thing.

Enjoying his role as a Texas-sized sugar daddy, Thayer expanded his leaking activities beyond LTV to other companies on whose boards he served. The first big opportunity came in June

1982, when, as a director of Anheuser-Busch, Thayer learned that the beer giant was considering a possible acquisition of four companies, including Dallas-based Campbell Taggart, a big baking concern. In the period between June 10 and June 22, Busch executives engaged in a flurry of activity concerning the prospective mergers. Meetings and telephone conversations among Busch, its lawyers and investment bankers, crisscrossed the country from St. Louis to New York to Washington to Dallas. The discussions came to a head at a June 23 board meeting, attended by Thayer, at which Campbell Taggart was identified as the prime acquisition candidate.

Convinced that Busch would proceed with an offer for Campbell Taggart, Thayer ran off at the mouth again, allegedly informing good old Billy Bob and girlfriend Ryno of the wisdom of buying shares in the Dallas baker. Knowing a good bet when she saw one, the SEC charged, Ryno purchased 2,000 Campbell Taggart shares at $25¾ and $26⅜ per share on June 30 and July 1. At the same time, Harris stored away 3,100 shares, bought at 26⅜, for the accounts of his father and stepmother.

Then the action heated up. On July 6 Thayer, who was vacationing in Canada, placed a five-minute call to Busch chairman August Busch III. Learning that management was about to meet with the corporation's lawyers and investment bankers for an eleventh-hour review of the Campbell Taggart acquisition, Thayer dialed Billy Bob with the news. The next day William Mathis reportedly took a 30,800 share in the likely takeover target.

The government claims that Mathis, in what had become a well-oiled party line, touted the stock to his own cronies. According to the SEC, "More than 100,000 shares of Campbell Taggart common stock were purchased by customers and associates of Mathis, or by persons known to such customers and associates."

The big payoff was now in sight. Before flying from Dallas to St. Louis on July 27 to attend a dinner with the Busch board of directors, to be followed the next morning by a formal board meeting, Thayer again spoke on the phone with Harris. That same day, Billy Bob resumed his acquisitions of Campbell Taggart common stock for his account and for those of his customers.

What looked like an odds-on wager quickly turned into a sure thing. On July 28 Busch's board of directors authorized management to engage in merger negotiations with Campbell Taggart. Exactly twenty-eight minutes after the board concluded its business, Thayer placed a five-minute call to Ryno from a pay phone in Brighton, Missouri.

The piranhas went into a frenzy. Between July 27 and July 30, Harris (and his friend, aerobic dance instructor Julie Williams), Ryno, Schroder, Davis, Sharp (and his friend, airline stewardess Julia Rooker) allegedly purchased 40,000 shares of Campbell Taggart stock on margin at prices ranging from 28¼ to 29½ per share.

On August 1 executives from Busch and Campbell Taggart met to negotiate the terms of a merger whereby Busch would acquire Campbell Taggart. Two days later the companies announced that they were holding preliminary negotiations and on August 9 that they had reached a merger agreement in which Busch would pay $36 per share for some of Campbell Taggart's common stock and would exchange convertible preferred stock for the remaining shares.

With the die cast, the Texas Rangers started unloading their shares. According to the SEC, Ryno took $21,145 in profits; Harris cleared $24,401; Schroder pocketed $5,254; Mathis, the big winner in this one, corralled $146,829. Harris sold shares purchased for his father and his cousin for profits of about $31,710 and $6,177.

A respectable haul, but not nearly enough to satisfy what had become runaway greed. Eager to cash in again, the trading ring allegedly went on to profit from Thayer's role as a director of Allied Corporation. Leaking word to friends and lovers about Allied's September 1982 tender offer for Bendix, Thayer helped the circle of insiders earn windfall profits of about $757,000.

There is an old Wall Street saying, however: "The bulls and the bears make money, but the pigs get gored." And just as the take was growing—and as some of the players were convinced they'd hit on the perfect crime—that saying caught up with the Thayer ring. The SEC had launched a ten-month investigation after detecting the preannouncement run-up in Bendix shares, and it now proceeded to shock Wall Street and Washington by charging Thayer with leaking confidential information. Then, before anyone could catch his breath, the U.S. Attorney's Office for the District of Columbia accused Thayer and Harris of obstructing justice, by charging they had given the SEC false testimony during the course of its investigation.

Though Thayer started off loudly proclaiming his innocence—stating in a January 1984 letter to President Reagan that the SEC allegation against him was "entirely without merit"—in March 1985 he would plead guilty to obstructing justice and his lawyers would beg U.S. District Court Judge Charles Richey for leniency. But there would be no mercy. Thayer and Harris would have to disgorge $825,000 in profits and would be sentenced to four years in jail. Sometime after Thayer and Harris were sentenced, the government would drop its case against Ryno, Sharp, Williams and Rooker. Schroder settled by paying back $176,383. Mathis and Davis, who have never been convicted of anything, are still contesting the government's charges. The man at the center of the case found that his life had changed the most.

"Thayer was stunned at the sentence," says a lawyer with experience in insider trading cases. "All along, he expected to get away without a jail sentence. Why? Because as a white-collar criminal—as a distinguished corporate director turned Pentagon bigwig—he thought he could manipulate the system. By hiring the right lawyer, paying some financial penalties and saying a few humble things, he thought he could stay scot-free.

"You see, Thayer thought he was smarter than the system. And he wasn't alone. That's what makes inside leakers leak and inside traders trade. And it's what makes them think they can get away with it.

"But in Thayer's case, it didn't work that way. Why? Because the government was intent on making an example of Thayer. By hooking a big fish—and by making him do time for his crime—it was hoping that others tempted to go the same route would think twice before they acted. But no way. Throughout the investigation, the pleading and the sentencing, others—some much bigger fish—were leaking and trading on a much grander scale. Some would be caught soon after. Others never would."

II

Rumor Mill

Gallows humor heard shortly after arbitrager Ivan Boesky agreed to pay $100 million in an insider trading case: "Did you hear how Boesky's going to pay his fine? He's putting up five million and Drexel Burnham's selling junk bonds for the rest!"

Paul Thayer the corporate director stands as a classic symbol of the insider who got caught. As key members of the management team, the CEO, the directors and other senior executives participate in all of the corporation's secret deliberations; they are instrumental in shaping its plans and learn of material actions well in advance of public announcements. Thus, when the SEC identifies trading anomalies in a company's stock—when it is clear that someone is playing with a stacked deck—the managers and directors emerge as prime suspects. It is as if they were encased in neon. To some, including much of the general public, it's an open-and-shut case.

If only it were that simple. What makes insider trading so complex, so pervasive, is that word of corporate secrets leaks out through an extensive rumor mill that may begin with the most casual of contacts. In such instances, the originator of the leaks may have no official capacity with the company. Instead, he may be a friend or confidant to senior management. Such was the case with one Giuseppe Tome, a smooth and charming Italian who, according to the SEC, parlayed a personal friendship with Seagram chairman Edgar Bronfman into a blitz of insider trades that netted $3.5 million in illegal profits.

As the SEC put it at the time it filed suit: "We find a personal acquaintance that flowered and bloomed into an intimate friendship and a professional association in which trust and confidence were reposed in Tome, of which he callously took shoddy and unlawful advantage."

By all accounts, Tome was a whiz at the old Dale Carnegie goal of winning friends and influencing people. Starting out in the securities business in 1959 as a stockbroker in Bache & Company's Milan, Italy, office, he turned a flair for sales and internal politics into a series of promotions, culminating in the chairmanship of Bache & Company (Overseas), S.A., headquartered in Geneva, Switzerland. From there he moved to a senior international post with E. F. Hutton in 1973 and assumed responsibility for hundreds of stockbrokers operating out of twenty-two offices worldwide. He rose to the top again, becoming president of Hutton's international division and a member of its board of directors.

For Tome, whose expectations had risen along with his rank, high corporate office now appeared limited. Leaving Hutton in 1979, he launched his own firm, Compagnie pour le Financement et l'Investissement, S.A. (better known as Finvest Geneva), to engage in an ambitious program of stock and commodities brokerage, securities trading and underwriting, Eurobond transactions, currency management and investment banking.

If there was a financial transaction to be done, Finvest Geneva was positioned to do it. All that was left was for clients to believe in the company. From his Dale Carnegie track record, Tome knew he could take care of that.

The first big breakthrough came when Tome and his wife met Mrs. Bronfman at a social function in July 1980. Laying on his charm, Tome quickly befriended the spouse of one of the world's wealthiest men and made so vivid an impression that the Tomes were invited to join an exclusive party of fourteen friends flying later that month to attend a rodeo in celebration of Mrs. Bronfman's birthday.

A captive audience—it was as if Tome had written the script himself. Once aboard the Seagram corporate plane, he shifted his attention from Mrs. Bronfman to focus on her husband, Edgar, who just happened to be the chairman of the board of the giant company.

Forever the salesman, Tome engaged Bronfman in a conversation about international currency transactions, offering his opinion—or "insight," as he called it—that by keeping all of their accounts in U.S. dollars, American corporations were "going short" on other currencies. To avoid this, he suggested that those same companies maintain a portfolio of varied currencies. Adding weight to his advice, Tome produced—as if from thin air—a press clipping praising the speaker as an authority on currency strategies.

Smitten with this corporate Svengali and intrigued by his "insight" into currency holdings, Bronfman introduced Tome to Harold Fieldsteel, Seagram's chief financial officer, and then to a slate of company officers. In a memo to his executives prior to their meeting with Tome to discuss the company's currency position, Bronfman wrote that Tome's record warranted their "taking a serious look at his firm's capabilities."

Once he was blessed with this kind of introduction, it was child's play for the skillful Tome to close in on both Seagram and its chairman. In less than three months after his first introduction to Bronfman, Finvest had snared Seagram as a major client.

Two deals were signed. Under the terms of a "Foreign Exchange Advisory Agreement," Finvest would advise Seagram on world currencies and would help the corporation form a foreign-exchange advisory committee—whose members were to be selected by Finvest. Soon afterward, Seagram inked another agreement, authorizing Finvest to place $10 million of Seagram's money in a portfolio of currencies, bonds and notes—changing, as it saw fit, from one currency to another.

By the time the second deal was signed, Bronfman had come to view Tome—whom, by all objective standards, he barely knew—as "a sort of European consultant to Seagram generally." It was in this context of trust and privilege that the chairman began soliciting Tome's opinion on Seagram's secret plans to make a number of corporate acquisitions. Considering Tome an experienced financial executive familiar with the rules of confidentiality, Bronfman made him privy to a stream of proprietary information.

"Unquestionably, Tome was Bronfman's friend and adviser, had formal contractual relationships with Seagram, through Finvest Geneva, and had vast experience in the securities industry," the SEC charged in its court filings. "Clearly, he was looked upon and treated by Bronfman as an insider of Seagram, as he had become."

Bronfman's trust in Tome extended to his personal finances as well. The chairman opened a Finvest account for trading commodity futures and currencies, gave his Italian confidant power of attorney and personal discretion over the assets, and even joined with him as an investor in the Broadway musical *Sophisticated Ladies*. On the social front, the Tomes and the Bronfmans cultivated a budding friendship, hosting each other at a series of exotic rendezvous that provide a revealing glimpse into the extravagant life-styles of the rich and powerful.

In November 1980 the Bronfmans jetted off to a majestic weekend at Tome's ski lodge in Mageve, France. On the same trip, the group moved en masse to Switzerland, where they attended a dinner party at Tome's Geneva residence. A month later, Tome kicked off the hunting season in grand style by visiting the Bronfmans at their Charlottesville, Virginia, mansion. And to toast the new year, the couples—now clearly a mutual admiration society—sunned themselves on a yacht floating off the coast of Mexico.

While all of this wining and dining and tanning was going on, Seagram, which had recently sold its interest in Texas Pacific Oil Company for $2.3 billion, was on the prowl for "attractive investments," a euphemism for undervalued companies. Going about this scientifically, management set up a committee to identify attractive candidates, commissioned the consulting firm of Arthur D. Little to study how the world would change in the next two or three decades (and thus where the best business opportunities would lie) and arranged a $3 billion line of credit to finance a monster takeover.

Sniffing opportunity in Seagram's cash balances, Tome started probing deeper into the company's internal affairs. With the chairman trusting him, he needed only push a button and the doors would open wide. Requesting that Seagram provide him with a general briefing on its policies, operations and finances, he got that and more. Bronfman spoke with him directly and informed the "consultant" of the corporation's acquisition plans, including those for hostile tender offers.

Immediately, Tome linked his investment moves to Seagram's "secret" corporate strategies. In the fall of 1980, for example, Seagram considered buying up as much as 20 percent of Texaco's outstanding shares. As the corporation pursued its plans, Finvest became a heavy buyer of Texaco, which proved to be Finvest's most heavily traded stock in November and December of that year. Once Bronfman decided against a full-blown tender offer for Texaco, Finvest—with its ear to the chairman's office—began dumping the oil company's stock, its action coming immediately after Bronfman's about-face.

Later that month, while Tome was visiting with Bronfman in Charlottesville, he learned that the chairman and his acquisition committee were making eyes at Sante Fe Industries, one of several companies with massive coal reserves that Bronfman believed would prove very valuable in the future.

As Bronfman recalled the conversation, Tome asked whether Seagram had gotten any closer to making a decision about what the company was going to do about an acquisition. Bronfman replied, "Yes, I think we are looking very hard at Sante Fe."

When he asked if a date had been set for the Santa Fe deal, Tome was informed that investment bankers Goldman Sachs and Lazard Frères were advising Seagram on the matter and that it would take another few months to put the pieces together. Soon after, Finvest began accumulating Santa Fe shares, commencing a buying binge that lasted from late December 1980 to early January 1981.

Though Tome had moved deeper and deeper into Seagram's confidences, Bronfman saw no reason to warn his friend/adviser/consultant of the need to respect what he'd learned as inside information. As the chairman put it:

"I didn't think it was necessary [because of Tome's] twenty years in the business. He ought to know the rules. I assume he does know the rules . . . that basically [what I told him] was inside information"—materially nonpublic information.

Guided by this blind faith—which is at the heart of a shocking number of corporate security programs—Seagram continued to reveal itself like an open book. For Tome, it was an opportune time to eavesdrop on the corporation. The hunt for takeover prey was growing more intense.

At a Seagram board meeting held by conference call on January 13, 1981, management was authorized to invest up to $150 million in four companies—all potential acquisition targets. Although the board was not told of the names until its next regularly scheduled meeting on February 4, Tome already knew—from previous discussions with Bronfman—that the targets included Sante Fe, Amax and St. Joe. A fourth, Kimberly-Clark, was added to the list but was never a serious candidate.

Two weeks later, Sante Fe was scratched from Seagram's acquisition plans—word of which was conveyed to Tome. In short order, Finvest began selling Sante Fe shares.

To this point, all the inside information had led to dead ends. But the good stuff was just around the corner and Tome, like any good investor, had patience.

The list narrowed quickly. Next to go was Amax. With 20 percent of that corporation's shares held by Standard Oil of California (Socal), Seagram dispatched the investment banking firm Lazard Frères to inquire if Socal would sell its stake. Informed that the oil giant was holding onto its shares, thank you, Seagram shelved the idea of going after Amax.

According to Bronfman, that, "almost by a process of elimination, left St. Joe." Although Bronfman never recalled telling Tome that Amax was a dead issue, Socal's own tender offer for the company, which came on March 6, 1981, all but ruled out a Seagram bid for it. Thus, in early March, an astute observer of Tome's caliber would likely know, on the basis of his confidential knowledge of Seagram's original shopping list, that only one viable target remained.

By then Seagram had decided to proceed with a tender offer for St. Joe. After a favorable report from Lazard Frères, Bronfman flashed the green light on February 25, 1981. Every effort was made to keep the company's intentions from leaking out to the marketplace. Even Tome, it seems, was not informed of the go-ahead. If the routine pattern of trading in St. Joe stock was any indication, the lid of secrecy appeared to be fastened securely. Concerned that it stay that way, Lazard Frères recommended speeding up the takeover timetable and Bronfman agreed.

At his New York office on March 9—shortly before a critical meeting with the Seagram takeover team—Bronfman spoke on the phone with Tome, then visiting in New York, who said he was calling to invite the chairman to dinner the following evening. Declining, Bronfman informed Tome that he would be in Montreal for a directors' meeting.

The wheels in Tome's mind apparently started spinning. Knowing that the acquisition candidates had been winnowed down to one serious contender, that some kind of corporate action was imminent and that Bronfman was jetting off to a board meeting the following day, Tome apparently recognized that a play for St. Joe was in the works. He wasted no time in taking a share of the action. According to the SEC, Tome began frenzied buying of St. Joe call options and stock and tipped others to do the same.

"Tome's immediate conduct confirmed that he was not merely speculating on what was afoot," U.S. District Court Judge Milton Pollack stated in his opinion. "The extraordinary scope of his financial activities on the next morning was beyond any notion of rational, normal trading. The facts and circumstances lead to the ineluctable inference, which the court draws, that Tome had obtained material nonpublic information in confidence from Seagram that it intended to make a tender offer for St. Joe."

Beginning at 8:55 A.M. on March 10—just hours after speaking with Bronfman and before the Seagram board would meet—Tome, apparently trying to camouflage his actions, placed overseas orders for St. Joe call options to be executed on the Philadelphia exchange. The purchases were made for the accounts of three Panamanian companies Tome controlled. In addition, Tome made at least fourteen telephone calls to European clients and business associates, advising them to get in on the St. Joe bonanza.

But this was just the hors d'oeuvre. As the day went on, Tome continued his supermarket sweepstakes, placing a series of orders through Banca Della Svizzera Italiana (BSI), the Swiss-based institution that maintained his trading accounts, and tipping still others to follow suit. When the market closed on March 10, Tome and his piggyback purchasers had allegedly gobbled up options on at least 185,000 shares of St. Joe stock and made outright purchase of 60,500 shares of St. Joe common.

On March 10 Seagram secretly authorized the St. Joe tender offer and then made the news public after a board meeting on March 11. With the machinery for a takeover set in motion, Bronfman returned from Montreal to New York to join his wife and the omnipresent Tome for a previously scheduled date to attend a performance of *Sophisticated Ladies*. That evening, Bronfman confided to Tome elaborate details of the St. Joe tender offer, including Seagram's strategy, its pricing and its chances for success. Throughout, Tome was "eloquently silent and mentioned absolutely nothing to Bronfman about Tome's orders, trades, telephone calls overseas, and exhortations to others in regard to St. Joe securities," according to Judge Pollack's opinion.

From all indications, Bronfman was thoroughly duped.

On March 12 the chairman held a dinner party at his home in Tome's honor. Again he talked at length about the St. Joe offer, and again Tome, the cigar-store Indian, said nothing of his St. Joe purchases. Convinced that he had outfoxed the system—that his Panamanian corporations and Swiss bank accounts would shield him—he enjoyed the good food and drink, content in the knowledge that he was getting richer by the hour.

But what at first appeared the perfect crime soon revealed itself to be flawed. Here too, the "pigs get gored" rule would come into play.

The day after the dinner party, as Tome began to unload his St. Joe options, the SEC—which had been startled by a run-up in St. Joe volume and prices just before the tender offer was announced—declared that it was launching an inquiry into possible insider trading in St. Joe shares. Scheduled to stay at his New York hotel until March 18, Tome grabbed the next widebody for Switzerland, returning there on March 14. In Geneva the following day, according to government charges, Tome tried to arrange a cover-up, asking BSI executives to doctor the option purchases so as to camouflage Finvest's involvement. But the bank flatly refused.

The SEC, which had traced the St. Joe trading to certain BSI accounts maintained in New York at Irving Trust, could not find out who controlled the accounts. Citing Swiss secrecy laws, BSI refused to name names.

To pierce this cover—one that had long stymied investigations on insider trading—on March 27, the SEC filed suit naming BSI as the only defendant and asking that the accounts of "unknown purchasers" be frozen at Irving Trust. In this way, $1,825,000 of the proceeds of the insider trading—along with BSI's considerable assets in the United States—would be impounded.

Although Tome's name was not mentioned in the SEC's suit, Bronfman, suspicious of the Swiss connection, called Tome to learn if he had done anything. Bronfman recalled: "I wanted to make doubly sure he hadn't. Because the only person I knew in Switzerland that would have any knowledge one way or another of anything that was going on, at least from me, was Mr. Tome."

According to the court, Bronfman remembered the Italian telling him: "You know I've been in this business for twenty years and I know what to do and what not to do. And clearly, I certainly didn't do anything. . . . But it's a little more complicated than that, and I will see you in New York next week."

When the men did meet in person the following week—first alone and then in the presence of attorneys—Tome reiterated his innocence and claimed that an associate, hearing rumors about St. Joe, had placed an order for the stock without his knowledge.

In response to direct questions, Tome allegedly stated point-blank that neither he nor his family members had any beneficial interest in the St. Joe shares.

But the truth was revealed when, with the gun of frozen assets to its head, BSI revealed Tome's name. By that time, Tome had fled to Europe, where he remains a fugitive from justice.

Did Tome suffer for his crimes? Not really. Although the U.S. District Court for the Southern District of New York found Tome guilty of violating the nation's securities laws, he never served a day of time and his tippees retained millions of dollars in trading profits. For all intents and purposes, members of the Tome trading ring can view the St. Joe deal as a productive transaction. One man's friendship with the chairman of a major corporation had lined their pockets with the fastest money they had ever made.

Did the episode leave Bronfman, the easy mark in all of this, with a bitter taste, or a determination to take a harder line against inside leaks? Perhaps, but according to court papers, he had his wife call Tome's wife in April 1981 to tell her, "Don't worry. We love you. . . . The reason Edgar's not calling you is because he's been advised not to. But he still loves you."

The Tome case had effects far beyond the fate of one particular individual, however. Ira (Ike) Sorkin, former New York regional administrator for the SEC, says: "The case had a dramatic impact because it was the first time a federal judge—acting on an inside trading case—froze the assets of a Swiss bank in this country. Unless BSI complied, they knew they would lose their American assets and even more important would be unable to function in the U.S. With the multinational nature of bank transactions today, no major bank can be without a New York presence. The penalties for failing to reveal Tome's identity were too great for BSI to accept. So they told us who was doing the trading in St. Joe."

The news of Judge Pollack's order freezing the U.S. assets of

Banca Della Svizzera Italiana sent shock waves through the Bermuda Triangle of insider trading extending from New York to Zurich to the Bahamas.

At Bank Leu in Switzerland, word of the judge's action set off a chain reaction resulting in a flurry of messages between the home office in Zurich and the Nassau outpost. The bottom line of the messages: we may have an insider of our own.

In secret testimony given years later to the SEC, Bank Leu's general manager for the Bahamas, Bruno Pletscher, recalled receiving a copy of a *Wall Street Journal* article on Judge Pollack's freeze order. It came directly from Bank Leu executive J. P. Fraysse, then head of the Nassau office:

SEC: "Is it your understanding that the *Wall Street Journal* article relates to a lawsuit instituted by the Securities and Exchange Commission relating to possible trading on inside information?"

Pletscher: "My understanding at the time was that Banca Della Svizzera Italiana was involved, or was involved through one of their customers, in an insider trading situation, and the memo given to me I understand as a message that we should avoid becoming involved in an insider trading inquiry."

SEC: "An inquiry by the Securities and Exchange Commission?"

Pletscher: "Yes."

SEC: "The first paragraph of the memo reads as follows: 'Mr. J. P. Gabriel said in Miami that the SEC was getting very tough on insiders and that we have to be very careful if we have *clients sailing a bit too close to the wind*.' . . . Did you understand clients 'sailing a bit too close to the wind' to refer to *clients who might be trading on inside information*?"*

---

*Here and throughout in transcripts of testimony before the SEC, emphasis has been added by the author.

Pletscher: "Yes, I was aware of the point that was mentioned in the same paragraph, that we have 'one,' meaning we have one client, who has executed orders through our bank and has traded in securities that effectively were involved in a takeover situation, and that the client in most of these cases was obtaining a big profit out of his trades. *It was my understanding that this client might have information that could be categorized as insider information.*"

That client was Dennis Levine. At the time Tome and his satellite traders were buying and selling St. Joe, Dennis Levine had already amassed more than a quarter-million dollars in the secret account he had opened in May 1980 in Bank Leu's Nassau, Bahamas, branch under the code name Mr. Diamond. Abusing his insider position as a Smith Barney investment banker and sharing information with fellow investment banker Robert Wilkis, then with Lazard Frères, Levine had used confidential knowledge of corporate acquisitions and buyouts to profit from at least half a dozen stocks.

His story will be told shortly. But first, what was the purpose of the Bank Leu memo? To alert the Bahamian staff to a law enforcement problem? To serve as a catalyst for corrective action? Just the opposite. Bank Leu's apparent objective was to conceal rather than report Levine's insider trading activity, as is evident from the full text of the memo:

MEMORANDUM

To: C. Schlatter

From: J. P. Fraysse

Date: 10th April, 1981.

Ref: Article from *Wall Street Journal* dated 30th March on the SEC action against Banca Della Svizzera Italiana (Overseas) Ltd.

Mr. J. P. Gabriel said in Miami, that the SEC was getting very tough on insiders and that we had to be quite careful if we had clients sailing a bit too close to the wind. We have one.

As a precaution, in future, we should underline to potential clients the risk involved in such dealings which can result in the freezing of the assets of BLI [Bank Leu International] in the USA and under prosecution to the disclosure of the client's name.

As a further precaution, if we feel that the order is excessive in amounts, or in number of shares, compared to the daily volume of such securities in New York, we should take the initiative of reducing it. Perhaps we should also avoid using Europartners, which is controlled by foreign institutions. In any case, such transactions should be kept under constant review and any new orders should be immediately reported to me.

J. P. Fraysse

cc: B. Pletscher
    D. A. Benjamin

Enc.

Note that there is no shock—and certainly no moral outrage—at finding an inside trader operating under the auspices of an ostensibly reputable bank. Instead of turning the suspect in, the call is to camouflage his securities purchases by reducing the orders and replacing New York–based Europartners with another broker likely to assume a lower profile. If Bank Leu found something wrong, immoral or unethical about insider trading—or about the bank's role in it—certainly the memo did not express it.

The only imperative, one shared by dozens of elite financial institutions that have shielded inside traders in one way or another, was to *avoid getting caught*.

"But eventually that would prove impossible," says SEC attorney Robert Blackburn, who prosecuted the Tome case. "Impossible for Bank Leu, for Dennis Levine, and for Ivan Boesky. Why? Because years later, when the government tied Bank Leu to insider trading, they had to reveal Levine's name or face the same gun we put to the head of Banca Della Svizzera Italiana. The Tome case made it clear that the U.S. would not tolerate concealment of inside traders—and would take tough action against those who did. Bank Leu knew it had to cooperate or face drastic sanctions. So the bank would sing on Levine, and Levine would sing on Boesky, and on and on.

"If you want to know the reason we were able to uncover the recent crop of inside traders, you have to look to the Tome case. It was the crack in the dam that made all the rest possible. Tome didn't end insider trading—there were many more cases to come—but it gave us the heavy artillery to go after the biggest and most devious traders on the Street. And we set about doing just that."

III

A Creature of the Street

"Dennis could have been a successful gigolo, but he wanted Wall Street instead."
  —JACK FRANCIS, *former professor of Levine's at Baruch College*

The Tome breakthrough, unleashing as it did a new weapon
for the SEC, couldn't have come at a better time. By the
early 1980s, the potential for insider trading had reached
alarming proportions.

While the financial community has always been a magnet for
the fast-buck artists (and every generation has had its inside
traders) the Wall Street that made stars of Dennis Levine and
Ivan Boesky marked a new low in American capitalism. The decline of ethics and morality and gentlemanly business practices—which once had their place in the premier investment
banks—coincided with the shift of power in the corporate world
from the Fortune 500 chief executives to the takeover sharks who
prey on them.

With the rise of the new breed of entrepreneurial asset-shifters
like T. Boone Pickens, Saul Steinberg and Carl Icahn—men
whose Machiavellian tactics have produced billions in profits,
often for breaking up rather than building companies—investment banking changed to reflect these powerful new clients and
the practices they wrought. In many of the firms, Drexel Burnham Lambert chief among them, young men learned that they
would rise quickly by trading the traditional white shoes for
spikes.

"The bright students who walk out of these doors on the way to
distinguished careers come in two basic models," says a dean at
New York's Columbia University. "The first, those I think of as

the more traditional group, want to transform their degrees into distinguished professional careers. They want to make money, yes, but they also want the prestige, and perhaps the collegiality, that a profession affords. So they tilt toward medicine and the law. Once down that road, they have to comply with a set of rules—technical and ethical—that the profession enforces on its members. In ten years or so, they'll have the satisfaction of achieving professional competence and the income and recognition that go with that.

"An interesting and rewarding life. Who can argue that? Only the other brand of students, to whom the thought of such a career is about as appealing as a stint in the infantry. What puts them off? Everything. The slow build, the rules, the ethics, and the limits (even surgeons have them) on personal earnings.

"To this group, Wall Street is the promised land. Learning that they can go directly to the investment banks, parlaying a feel for finance into a million dollars a year—in the time it takes a young surgeon to learn operating-room etiquette—is all they have to hear. Their entire college careers are structured simply to get a foot in the door of the Drexel Burnhams of the world. They want and expect staggering sums of money without the career progression and the professional standards that would ordinarily go with that. And in recent years, Wall Street's hung out a neon sign that announces to them, in so many words: 'That's what you can expect here. Make a lot of money and no one's going to ask questions.'"

Says a Wall Street attorney with the firm of Sullivan & Cromwell (whose former office manager, accounting clerk and purchasing manager were found guilty of insider trading in 1985), "The new Wall Street, as typified by Drexel, takes its cues, and its fees, from a bunch of shady guys who found out they could take over companies by spotting a weakness in those companies, rounding up a pool of money—mostly from Drexel—and talking tough.

"Although they often try to dress up their actions with talk of stockholder rights and the like, these guys couldn't give a shit about anything but their own bank accounts. They shun manners, etiquette, principles—all the things that for years kept Wall Street from becoming the jungle that it now is. To accommodate these men—to prove they're as crass and ruthless as their clients—some of the investment banks have sunk to their level. By that I mean going out and grabbing for bucks without any concern about what their actions will do to Wall Street, to the stock markets, to capitalism. And they've made it clear to the people who want to work for them that that's the new religion. Or should I say the new atheism."

In every way, Dennis Levine reflected this modern Wall Street. A compulsive liar with a voracious appetite for the quick buck, he conned his way to the top of a twisted business that asks only how much you can make for it today without regard for how you make it. Who it is you rape or plunder is immaterial. Again, the universal rule is "Don't get caught."

It was in this environment that Dennis Levine thrived, building an insider network, trading under the table, lying whenever necessary—all without arousing a hint of suspicion on the part of his superiors, men with decades of experience on the Street. How can that be explained? In three ways: first, no one really cares about insider trading (providing you "don't get caught"); second, there are no real controls to prevent it; and third, the cultivation of inside information is so pervasive on takeover-crazed Wall Street that careers, livelihoods and reputations depend on it.

While inside information has always been valuable, the nature of that information—and what can be done with it—has changed, making it more valuable than ever. In the past, if an insider learned that Warner-Lambert, the pharmaceutical house, was close to developing a miracle cure for the common cold, the payoff for that scoop would come months or more likely years later, when and if the cure was announced. By then, speculation would have gradually nudged the stock to new highs.

But in the takeover era, inside information has been transformed from material news of a company's internal operations to the knowledge that it is the subject of a tender offer, à la St. Joe or Campbell Taggart. Gaining advance news here can mean almost instant profits—tens of millions of dollars in a matter of days or hours. That is precisely why the effort to gain inside information has corrupted some of the Street's most prominent figures; why Ivan Boesky, the arbitrage community's major-domo, was willing to engage in an illegal relationship with Dennis Levine, a minor player by Boesky's standards. Levine had something—inside information—that Boesky was willing to pay to get. With little but greed to bind them, they became, in a sense, business partners. One of dozens, perhaps hundreds, of similar partnerships that run like a secret subway beneath the streets of lower Manhattan.

In fact, Levine's rise to wealth and power in a world controlled by the Boeskyites is the pluperfect example of how a young man, driven only by greed and ambition, could make it big on a Wall Street obsessed with gaining and trading information. His secret was that he saw the financial community for what it had become: a lawless culture willing to pay a hefty bounty for confidential data.

But where did Levine come from? How did he rise by the age of thirty-three to a Wall Street partnership and a million-dollar-a-year salary? The story begins in Bayside, New York, a middle-class Shangri-La not far from Archie Bunker's blue-collar ghetto in the borough of Queens. Although it was just an hour's bus and subway ride to Long Island City, across the East River and then down to Wall Street, no one in the neighborhood young Dennis grew up in talked much about the stock market, save to check on an occasional hot tip passed along by the dry cleaner's brother-in-law or the periodontist's nephew.

Instead, the talk on the streets, in the high school and shopping centers, focused on personal achievement, on upward mobility, on making it through the respectable and seemingly guaranteed professions of law and medicine. In what was a patent career path, a young man would excel academically, gain admission to the Ivy League (Brandeis was an acceptable substitute), advance to graduate school and emerge eight years later with a piece of parchment and the economic insulation that it afforded. Such was the middle-class campus-to-profession career route that had become an article of religious faith since the Depression. But not for Dennis. From the beginning, he was a rebel.

A popular but so-so student who muddled his way through high school thinking more about his motorcycle and his girlfriends than his future, Dennis graduated from high school in 1970 with little appetite for higher education. Unlike his peers on 208th Street, who packed their trunks for the hallowed institutions of the early seventies, Levine circled Bayside in a holding pattern, failing at first to make the transition from high school to career, to independence.

To young Dennis, whose view of success was formed through the family's aluminum-siding business, entrepreneurship rather than academics held out the greatest promise. Like his father, Dennis knew that his natural-born talent was more along the line of Dale Carnegie than in scoring high in Philosophy 101. The challenge was in finding some way to harness that talent without following his brother Robert into the family business, a calling he considered beneath his station.

"Dennis eventually went to college, but only because he didn't know what else to do," says Jack Francis, a professor at New York's Baruch College, where Levine earned his undergraduate and MBA degrees. "At first he was unfocused, unsure of why he was really there. But then in his junior year or so he started developing an interest in Wall Street—which he identified as the place to make a lot of money. By his senior year, he was obsessed with the idea."

Learning of an elite breed of professionals who work behind the scenes, merging companies, acquiring others and raising millions of dollars in the process, Levine was captivated. These dealmakers, as the investment bankers were called, operated in a way that Dennis understood instinctively: rather than follow a finished script, the best of them wrote the rules as they went along. Like barracudas in the corporate waters, they operated within the establishment but were never really subject to its rules. In the name of a deal, they could stretch limits on moral and ethical behavior, in the process claiming platinum fees and swaggering reputations. Investment banking offered the promise of a breathless ascent to the Everest of power and wealth. Just what Dennis was after.

The more Levine explored the field, the more he found himself drawn to it. It was not uncommon, he learned, for young men still shy of thirty to earn $500,000, maybe $1 million a year, to drive Jaguars and Porsches, live in Park Avenue co-ops and dine nightly at Le Cirque. Getting to Wall Street, it seemed, was like waking up Christmas morning in a Newport mansion.

But there was a rub. A young man first had to get in the door. And for Dennis that posed a major problem. With investment banking having emerged as *the* glamour profession for the best and the brightest of the post-Vietnam, pro-business, let's-make-money, tail-end-of-the-baby-boom generation, the firms were inundated with a legion of applicants who had "Eagle Scout," "Princeton" and "cum laude" embossed on their resumés. Faced with this competition, Levine would have little more than a prayer of landing one of the handful of entry-level jobs available among the top Wall Street firms.

"Investment bankers consider themselves 'The Chosen,'" says the managing partner of a venerable Wall Street law firm that has served the investment banks since the original dealmakers came to America from Eastern Europe. "For the most part, they are guys who've succeeded since kindergarten. In every grade, through elementary, middle school, high school, college and graduate school, they were at the top. One young man who worked for us for a year before going across the street to an investment bank—a move that infuriated me because we'd met about a half dozen of his special demands just to hire him—told me at lunch one day that in his family, not only were B's unacceptable, they were a disgrace. So after suffering through his first B in eighth grade, he made it a point never to sink to such depths again. Straight A's the rest of the way. That, in part, is why we hired him and that's why the bankers grabbed him away.

"We have high standards at this firm—I'll make no bones about that—but over there it's unforgiving. Many of the investment bankers reviewing the resumés that come into their firms have never failed at anything. They want to make sure that those who work by their sides are cut from a similar cloth. That's why a guy who knocks on the door from a run-of-the-mill school—no matter how well he's done there—isn't likely to gain entry.

"To the archetypal nose-in-the-air investment banker, having gone to a pedestrian college is in itself a sign of failure. Next case."

After earning his MBA from Baruch in June 1976, Levine—driven by his lust for Wall Street and the aroma of the millions he heard were being made there—set out to win a place in investment banking, his mediocre credentials a challenge to be overcome. Convinced that if he could land interviews he could land a job, he bought banker's pinstripes, had his resumé professionally typed and arranged interviews up and down the Street. The same outgoing, breezy personality that had always charmed teachers and girlfriends and Baruch professors would, he hoped, work similar magic on Wall Street.

But within days, the wind was out of his sails.

"The brash young Ivy types who'd interview Dennis seemed to take great pleasure in denigrating his background and his academic credentials," Francis recalls. "After several of these painful experiences, we developed a strategy for dealing with the snobs.

"When wise-asses would point out that Baruch's entrance requirements were lower than the Ivy's, or that Baruch was not 'in the same universe as a Harvard,' Dennis would smile sweetly and respond: 'I hope you hire people for the work they do rather than for the school they went to.'

"Still, the offers never materialized. Why? Because once his resumé got past the interviewers, once it was circulated to others in the firms—others Dennis didn't have the opportunity to meet—the lack of Ivy credentials killed him. He just didn't look as good on paper as he did in the flesh."

From Water Street to Broad, from Pine to Maiden Lane, whether it was the fault of his lackluster credentials or his tendency to overcompensate for them, Levine struck out. The Berlin Wall of investment banking proved more formidable than Levine's disarming personality. He would have to find another route to the land of milk and honey.

"If nothing else, Dennis has always been a survivor," says a former friend, who recalls that learning of Dennis's arrest was like hearing of a death in the family. "Tell him he's down, that he can't do something, and he'll find a way to prove you wrong.

"So when Wall Street wouldn't have him on the strength of his parchment, that wasn't the end of the world. It was just time to unveil his back-door strategy: earn his stripes in a related field and enter investment banking from the rear."

With this in mind, in February 1977 Levine accepted a position in commercial banking with Citibank's corporate counseling department, a hot spot for banking up-and-comers. Hired as a $365-a-week management trainee, Levine worked on international cash management systems, capital budgeting and the analysis of corporate hedging strategies. Here he befriended a corps of ambitious peers, including Robert Wilkis, also a middle-class kid, but one who had gone to Harvard and Stanford Business School.

Viewing the Citibank job as little more than a turnstile to investment banking, Levine worked there only long enough—thirteen months—to add real-world experience to his resumé. Having proven his aptitude for financial derring-do in Citibank's labyrinthine international department, he put his curriculum vitae out to market again, crossing his fingers that the commercial bank stint would make up for his half-baked scholastics.

He hit paydirt—of sorts. Smith Barney, Harris Upham & Co., an old-line investment bank, liked the look of his resumé and granted Levine an interview. Having daydreamed about this moment since his undergraduate years—and having rehearsed just how he would handle himself when and if the opportunity presented itself—Levine performed well, bombarding his prospective saviors with 100,000 watts of charm, a buoyant smile and a steely self-confidence the bankers found impressive. He was hired in April 1978.

With this success came Dennis's first lesson in the ways of Wall Street: he learned that tough, hard-nosed Wall Street wasn't as tough and hard-nosed as it was cracked up to be. As long as things looked good on the surface, no one bothered to look beneath the veneer. One could stretch the truth and get away with it.

In a "please hire me" letter to a Smith Barney first vice-president, Levine boasted in the opening sentence of his "background in both mergers and acquisitions and international financial consulting." Clearly, the "mergers and acquisitions" part was more exaggeration than fact. Though Levine's work at Citibank may have touched on M&A deals, his experience in the field was slim at best. To define his college research, or his Citibank chores, as a "background" in mergers and acquisitions was more than a bit of hyperbole. But it worked—and Levine surely made a mental note of it.

"He had to see that his personality—always his most valuable asset—would serve him as well on Wall Street as it had done with his girlfriends and his buddies in Queens," says a friend who admired and envied Levine's infectious personality. "Even as an adult, as a young businessman, the knack was still there: he could make people believe in him."

Delighted with his coup, and with the evidence that his master plan for establishing a Wall Street career with charm and moxie was indeed proving out, Dennis celebrated—but with sparkling wine, not Dom Perignon. That would come later. From the start, he viewed the Smith Barney spot as transitional. A step in the right direction, but still just a step.

Two factors watered down the soup. First, though a respected investment bank, Smith Barney was not a real powerhouse in the mega—mergers-and-acquisitions arena that Levine knew offered the greatest promise of colossal fees and foolproof information.

The firm, famous for its commercials with John Houseman ("We make money the old-fashioned way. We *earn* it."), was a rung or two down the prestige ladder from Goldman Sachs, Salomon Brothers and First Boston. Second, and most distressing, Smith Barney ignored Levine's request for a place in the M&A department, exporting him instead to a corporate finance job in the firm's Paris office, where, a Smith Barney spokesman says, "he did the numbers crunching associates do." To a would-be Wall Street hotshot, it was like a sentence to Siberia.

"But it was just like Dennis to smile through it all, publicly at least, taking the job as a way to further wedge his impatient foot into the door of investment banking," says a former friend, who calls Levine "Mr. Wizard" for his uncanny ability to turn "what looked at first like tin into 14-karat gold." And, "It was just like Dennis to perform well—so well that they'd be forced to give him the M&A position he really creamed for."

Levine's work-reward formula was based on more than good faith. Before flying off to the City of Lights, Dennis sought and received a pledge from his new employer: should he do well in Paris, he'd be assured a ticket back and, finally, a spot in mergers and acquisitions.

With his supreme self-confidence, he knew it was just a matter of time. Put the champagne on ice.

In July 1979—a year and a month after leaving for Paris—Dennis and his wife, Laurie, returned to New York. Determined to segue immediately into M&A, Levine made a pest of himself with Smith Barney executives, reminding them like a broken alarm clock of their pledge to make a place for him in mergers and acquisitions. Within months they flashed the green light, as much to test his mettle as to get him off their backs. It was then that Levine officially joined the M&A department, capping a six-year drive that had begun during his second year at Baruch.

It was a joyous time for Dennis and Laurie. The vindication of a street-smart young man, initially rejected for his lack of Brahmin credentials, proved he could gain entry his own way. For Dennis, it was the ultimate test of a theory he'd applied all his life to girls and friends and family and jobs: if he wanted something badly enough—something that at first blush seemed beyond his reach—he could find a way to have it. And in seeking and gaining the prize, he could emerge with his reputation enhanced, a reputation for poise, verve and tenacity. Machiavelli was right, he would learn. Everyone loves a winner.

Or so it seemed.

Once firmly planted in Smith Barney's New York office—his first position of any consequence in the M&A business—Levine had time to observe his superiors, the first vice-presidents several years his senior and, higher still, the men who ran the firm and shared in its profit. Even to a young man indoctrinated in the Wall Street myth, it was an eye-opener.

"He went ga-ga at what he saw," says a former Drexel colleague who remembers Dennis's stories about the hungry years. "The awesome earning power—the handsome silk ties, the Cuban cigars, the $200 lunches—was greater than even a Wall Street worshipper could anticipate. Although Dennis wore respectable clothes—$150 suits he probably picked up at Macy's—guys maybe a year or two older were turned out in hand-sewn English chalk stripes at $750 a pop.

"And the limousines. God, I don't think anything turned his head like the banks of limos that would snake around the Street at quitting time, waiting to usher all those guys in the British suits home to Park Avenue duplexes and Greenwich colonials. Though Dennis was making more money at Smith Barney than he expected to make at that point in his career—and though he was pleased with the salary when he first landed the job—it quickly shrank in his eyes to a pittance, an embarrassment. After all, his suits were still off the rack, and the closest he got to a limo was a Yellow cab."

In short, Levine fell victim to the kind of soaring expectations that leave many of Wall Street's young professionals dissatisfied with what to the sane world are enormous salaries. Operating in a culture in which money is the only measure of a person's worth, and exposed as they are to staggering displays of wealth by colleagues and clients alike, they feel compelled to keep fueling their earnings—not by the 5 to 10 percent a year that give most Americans cause to cheer, but to double and triple them over and over again, as if they were immune to the bounds of fiscal reality.

"One thing that really rubbed Dennis the wrong way, I mean really gnawed at him," the former Drexel colleague recalls, "is that his clients made more money than he. From the earliest days of his career to the time he rose to become an investment banking partner, he bitched endlessly that while he was earning in the six figures, his clients were making nine. 'Next to them,' Dennis used to say. 'I feel like a pisher.'"

He wasn't the only one. Take the case of a man known fictitiously as Robert K., a mergers-and-acquisitions vice-president in his early thirties. Having landed at a major Wall Street firm after earlier stints at two smaller investment banks, he now serves as the number-two man on a series of major-league M&A deals, earns in the mid to high six figures, has an unlimited expense account, flies only first-class, charters planes when he's late, takes bungalows at the Beverly Hills Hotel (formerly owned by Ivan Boesky), rents Ferraris rather than Fords and has a house charge at the exclusive French restaurant La Côte Basque.

But it's not enough. Because success has come so fast and furious—because the firm's enormous fees make it possible to reward young bankers far in excess of their real contribution to clients, to the economy, to society in general—he expects more and more and more. Clearly, Wall Street has distorted his view of the world.

Asked about his career objectives, he reveals a plan to leave his current employer. Why?

"Because they're stealing my talent here—taking it for free. Last week, in a deal I engineered, one of my clients made forty-three million dollars. Shit, do you know how much I get out of that? Maybe another hundred thousand for my bonus. And I won't even get that till Christmas. It's embarrassing."

A hundred thousand dollars for a few weeks' work. Embarrassing? What will he do to top it?

"Do deals myself. I've got a friend at [the law firm] Skadden Arps. He knows the legal side, I know the business side. Together we'll find opportunities, raise the financing, buy the companies, break them up and make some real money. Hell, it's about time I got into the plus column. Do you realize I'm going to be thirty-five soon? What the hell do I have to show for it?"

Gripped by the same impatience for wealth, Levine embarked on a different route. One that five years later would land him in a federal prison. It began in earnest on May 27, 1980, the day Levine lied to his Smith Barney colleagues, saying he was going to visit his father-in-law, and to his wife, saying he was going on a business trip, and flew to Nassau in the Bahamas to open a secret brokerage account in the name of Mr. Diamond, for the express purpose of trading on inside information. At the time, Diamond's true identity was known only by Bank Leu.

In secret testimony given later to the SEC (still before it revealed Levine's name), Bank Leu's general manager Bruno Pletscher recalled the opening of the account.

> *SEC:* "Since approximately May of 1980 has there been a particular customer of Bank Leu who has directed trading activity in the securities listed on Exhibit 1 [a document containing a list of companies]?"
>
> *Pletscher:* "Yes. . . ."
>
> *SEC:* "How did you come to learn of the opening of this account?"
>
> *Pletscher:* "I have been told by the managing director, Mr. Fraysse, that such an account was acquired."
>
> *SEC:* "When did he tell you that?"
>
> *Pletscher:* "At the end of May 1980. . . ."
>
> *SEC:* "For the purposes of this proceeding, since we are not going to be inquiring about the name of this customer, why do we not refer to this customer as Mr. X, or if it is convenient 'the customer' or 'the client'? . . . Do you

know what nationality the customer is: Mr. X?"

Pletscher: "It came to my attention through the opening form that on the form it is indicated that the client is a U.S. citizen. I have also seen a photocopy of a passport that was presented at the time of the opening of the account, and that passport states 'U.S. citizen.'"

SEC: "Did that photocopy of the passport also include a photograph of Mr. X?"

Pletscher: "Yes, it did."

SEC: "Have you personally seen Mr. X?"

Pletscher: "At a later date I have seen Mr. X and I have seen the passport, and they are identical."

SEC: "You mean the passport photo and Mr. X are identical?"

Pletscher: "Yes."

SEC: "What profession was Mr. X engaged in at the time of the opening of the account?"

Pletscher: "At the opening of the account I was not aware of the profession that Mr. X had."

SEC: "Did you subsequently learn what profession he had at the time that he opened the account?"

Pletscher: "Yes . . . I learn through certain documents that Mr. X was an investment banker."

Having established a mechanism for insider trading—and with it the potential for great wealth—Levine next focused on improving the quality of information he could process through it. That meant rising quickly through the ranks, landing one of the senior investment banking positions where deals and inside information originate.

But there was a problem. The unwritten rule at Wall Street's investment banks, especially in the merger-and-acquisition departments, is that you rise to the level of your first impression. Enter the firm as a minor player and for as long as you stay there you're bush-league. Move mountains, win clients, part the seas and you may get some credit, and some money, for it; but the first impression sticks. The talk in the hallways is: "Hey, Ferguson did good work on that one. How'd that happen?"

Just how the ball and chain of first impressions can stall careers became painfully obvious to Levine after his triumphant (or so he thought) return from Paris. To his superiors, Levine remained a green kid from Queens, a bit player in the firm's M&A department. Yes, he'd done some good work for Citibank, and yes, he'd fared well in France, but he'd never done a deal and he hadn't gone to Wharton and he'd never be anyone to reckon with.

Not that he'd be asked to leave. Every firm needs its share of grunts. The system depends on it. When a deal is in progress, the junior men and women ("associates" in the parlance of investment banking) do the analytical work. Assume company X wants to acquire company Y. It falls to the investment bankers to analyze Y, as well as the financial effects its acquisition will have on X. Numbers have to be crunched, publicly available information studied, research reports read and reviewed. It's enough to give anyone an Excedrin headache—precisely why the partners avoid it like the plague, lateraling it off to the lowly associates who do the analysis, package it in a report, pass it to a technically oriented partner (called a "rocket scientist") who in turn punts it to another partner (rocket scientists are generally locked in the closet) for ultimate presentation to the client.

Because he'd begged his way into Smith Barney's M&A department as a virtual charity case, Levine feared that the snackles of first impressions would relegate his status to "permanent associate," or that his climb out of the cellar to partnership would take far longer than his personal timetable ("*rich* by age thirty-five")—or his inside trading needs—would allow.

It was in this period of concern over his fate at Smith Barney that Levine started assembling his own power base outside the firm, building bridges to the network of arbitragers that runs through every nook and cranny of Wall Street. Because he saw the arbs as fountains of information—and because he admired their ballsy, independent style—Levine was drawn to the arbs and they to him.

"The best arbs are twenty-four-hour-a-day manipulators, round-the-clock schemers and compulsive liars who'd tell their widowed mothers to bail out of a hot stock if they wanted to buy her position," claims a Salomon Brothers M&A partner who says he received and rejected Levine's resumé on two occasions— "because his dollar demands dwarfed his skill level." "The arbs saw the same slippery deceitfulness in Levine. In the convoluted logic that is the arbs' stock-in-trade, that was reason enough to trust him. He passed the arbs' litmus test: knowing him, they believed, and sharing news with him would put money in their pockets.

"For his part, Dennis thought that by building up his own network of contacts outside of Smith Barney, he'd be insulated from—or maybe even bigger than—the politics and the limitations the investment banks might impose on him. And of course he'd also be in better position to profit as an inside trader. The more he knew, he reasoned, the more money he'd make."

And there was also a hero complex at work.

"Hardly a day went by when Dennis didn't tell an arb story," says an investment banker and former Levine colleague. "To him they were larger than life. You know the way some guys talk about football or baseball stars: that's the way Dennis went on and on about the arbs, especially Ivan Boesky. When he'd read how much Boesky would make on a single trade—and how many millions he'd amassed in only a few years on Wall Street—well, it was like a grade-school kid reading Don Mattingly's batting exploits. He wanted to be like Boesky. To join him in the major leagues."

But it wouldn't happen at Smith Barney. Levine's concerns for his future at the firm proved well-founded when he was passed over for a vice-presidency (he was made only a second vice-president) in early 1981, nearly two years after returning from Paris. Unwilling to wait patiently for another turn, Levine stamped around the offices, creating tension between himself and M&A department head J. Tomlison Hill, a stickler for detail who is said to have viewed Levine's work as occasionally sloppy and technically weak. When it became apparent that this huffing and puffing was counterproductive, that in all likelihood it had permanently soured the relationship with Hill, Levine decided to leave Smith Barney.

Soon his resumé was on the Street again, this time with the all-important M&A credentials he'd lacked in previous go-rounds. Within weeks, he was snapped up by Lehman Brothers Kuhn Loeb, a half-WASP, half-Jewish firm that had seen a dramatic turnaround, going from the brink of bankruptcy to become one of the hottest firms on Wall Street. With its M&A business exploding faster than it could handle the workload, Lehman needed experienced bodies—on Wall Street that means two to three years—and Dennis appeared to fit the bill. That his technical skills were mediocre at best, that his work was occasionally sloppy and that he was denied a vice-presidency at Smith Barney had no impact on Lehman, which promptly appointed him a divisional vice-president. Once again his middle-class-boy-looking-for-a-break story worked like a charm.

"I was impressed with him," says Eric Gleacher, then head of Lehman's M&A department (now serving in the same capacity for Morgan Stanley). "He had an ambition, a fire in his belly. He told me about the Baruch College problem—that he didn't want that to hold him back—and that he hoped to become a great investment banker. Along with the others here who interviewed him, I thought he had potential and so I hired him. He looked like he'd be willing to work very hard."

Like others who hired Levine or worked closely with him, Gleacher has since erected a DMZ between himself and his former underling. Asked about unsubstantiated claims from other investment bankers that Levine was his protégé and that he tried to hire Levine at Morgan Stanley, Gleacher denies it all vehemently, adding that Levine was just another young investment banker in his department.

In gaining entry to Lehman Brothers—then at the epicenter of the M&A business—Levine gained further evidence that he could lie through his teeth and get away with it. In signing

Lehman's compliance form for new employees, Levine, already an inside trader through his Bank Leu account, agreed not to hold any securities accounts without Lehman's authority. But he was in violation of the pledge even before he put his pen to it. That he was deceiving a new employer apparently meant little to him. As little as this statement of ethics, to which he also signed his name:

Confidential nature of information

It is essential that all information concerning any business carried on in this office, whether security transactions or otherwise, should be kept completely confidential. The stock-in-trade of a banker is his integrity and his respect for the confidence that others place in him. There can be no excuse for failure to observe this fundamental principle.

Why did Levine willfully lie about his activities and his intentions, risking his future if his secret account and inside trading were discovered?

"Because he knew he wouldn't be discovered—not by Lehman or by other investment banks he might wind up working for," says a Wall Street attorney with thirty-three years of practice in the securities industry. "That's because those 'don't be a bad boy' forms the firms make everyone sign aren't meant to catch anyone. Hell, no. They're solely to make the firms look innocent if a bad boy gets caught. When asked why they didn't do anything to prevent this or that impropriety, the firms can respond with an 'Ah, but we did!' That's when they whip out the bad-boy form and say, 'Look, we told him not to do those things and he signed his name, swearing he wouldn't. You can't blame us if the guy's a compulsive liar.' That the firm did little to research the employee's background is not fit for discussion. Instead they just point to the form. A form that they know from the start is just a useless piece of paper. A form that never stopped anyone from doing anything."

Entering Lehman as a vice-president, Levine exchanged his image as a grunt for that of a "promising talent." But he didn't rest with that.

"As soon as he arrived, Dennis made a strategic decision about how he would conduct his career here," says a former colleague from the Lehman days. "He looked around and saw that the two entrenched M&A vice-presidents had skills he couldn't compete with. One was brilliant technically and the other was connected into the Lehman power establishment. So Dennis decided he had to find his own niche. And what was that? Monitoring the market, responding to developments before anyone else, and going out and getting business on that basis."

In short, Levine would refine the role he'd cultivated at Smith Barney, schmoozing with everyone in his path, extending his tentacles beyond the firm, doing favors and expecting favors in return. If he'd learned anything at this point in his career, it was that Wall Street operates on a "you scratch my back, I'll scratch yours" basis. He was determined to turn it into an art form—and in the process to turn business contacts into a network of inside sources.

Lawyers were high on his hit list. Involved in every major deal, often at the earliest and most secretive stages of negotiations, the M&A attorneys have two of Wall Street's most precious commodities: clients and information.

By building bridges to the premier law firms—principally Skadden Arps Slate Meagher & Flom and Wachtell, Lipton, Rosen & Katz—Levine hoped to cultivate sources that would tip him off to deals handled by a dozen or more investment banks. It was not a pipe dream. In spite of their image as pristine professionals, some lawyers were known to have their price. Bringing a key lawyer into his trading ring would be like pressing his ear to the wall at Goldman Sachs, Salomon Brothers, Morgan Stanley, Drexel Burnham, and Merrill Lynch. Whoever the law firms represented—and at one time or another Skadden Arps and Wachtell, Lipton represent just about everyone—he would know what they were up to before the news was made public.

On the career front—which he never forsook for his clandestine activities—Levine hoped to use his lawyer contacts to land clients for Lehman. He knew that in those M&A transactions in which corporate management approaches the investment banker first, and the banker in turn hires the attorney, the investment banker responsible for selecting the lawyers picks up an IOU from Messieurs Skadden, Arps, Wachtell, Lipton and the like. (Skadden Arps attorneys are not known to have played any role in the Levine trading ring.) Following the unwritten rule of Wall Street back-scratching, the lawyers would be wont to return the favor the next time a client came to them first in search of an investment banker.

"With this in mind, Dennis played the IOU route very creatively, very aggressively," says his former Lehman colleague. "He was smart enough, for example, to spread his referrals beyond Skadden and Wachtell. Every now and then he'd call in guys from Fried, Frank [Fried, Frank, Harris, Shriver & Jacobson, a New York law firm that would ultimately play a pivotal role in Levine's undoing], a solid M&A firm but not as prominent as Skadden and Wachtell. The idea was to build credits in every pocket of the Street.

"Also, when Dennis hired a law firm, he often called the senior partners directly. He wanted the top guys to know that Dennis Levine brought their firms business. Not that these legal legends were going to pass him inside information. He just hoped they would get to know him, think highly of him and take a turn scratching his back."

While polishing his schmoozing role at Lehman, Levine established himself as the point man for client relationships and, equally important, the guy people would remember when and if they wanted to trade information.

"Dennis knew from his Smith Barney days that in investment banking the heroes were the guys who could take some dry analytical report and deliver it to clients in a way that would leave them with their mouths wide open, drooling on their suits," says the former Lehman colleague. "Technical prowess meant squat. Regardless of who sat at some fucking computer assembling a report, the guy who presented it well—who could make show biz out of it—got all the credit.

"So while some of the VPs would get up to their asses in statistics and analyses and God knows what, Dennis wouldn't go near the stuff. Because he knew his talent was in selling this or that strategy, in standing before a room full of clients explaining why company X should acquire company Y, he let others do the work. He'd be the master of ceremonies. And he'd be the one people would remember."

But Levine was more than a showman. Playing the seamy underside of investment banking they don't teach at Wharton, he would work behind the scenes, manipulating market developments for the benefit of his client—and, most likely, for his secret trading account.

"While Dennis liked to play mystery man on this, he'd let on now and then that he was speaking to the arbs, starting rumors, making the other side think one thing was happening while the opposite was true," says the former Lehman colleague. "He was thin on the specifics, but by gluing together the pieces, I could get a feel for what he was up to.

"What do I think he did? Well, in the midst of a takeover, he'd get on the phone with the arbs and say, 'The situation is such that we are going to withdraw our bid.' Well, the other company's investment bankers hear this from the arbs, rethink their strategy, and maybe take their time doing something that needs immediate action. That's when Dennis strikes again, raising his bid and thus tightening the screws on the other side, just when they think they have breathing room. Then, to really confound his adversaries, he leaks word to the press that his client is about to take a certain action, knowing full well that nothing could farther be from the truth—that they intended to do just the opposite. His objective: to get the element of surprise. Dennis saw it as a war.

"You have to give Dennis credit. He accomplished what he set out to accomplish in his own inimitable way. He couldn't rely on old school ties. This wasn't a guy from Harvard or Yale. Nobody went to school where he did. He didn't grow up in the country clubs. He didn't have any of the traditional advantages. But that didn't stop him. He just created his own calling card. And what was that? Good information. An uncanny stream of good, reliable, money-making information."

Others who worked with Levine at Lehman, and later at Drexel, agree that he had a hotline to breaking news. Says another former co-worker:

"A deal would be happening and he'd know it would be happening before anyone else. In this business that kind of soothsaying makes a lot of friends. That's because the first investment bank to learn of a deal is usually the one that winds up handling it.

"Take Burroughs, a Lehman client when Dennis was at the firm. Burroughs would use Salomon, Goldman and us—depending, quite often, on who brought the idea or the deal to them. If we called and said that we'd learned through our sources that undervalued XYZ Corporation was about to be acquired by a shark, but that Burroughs could queer the deal and take the prize itself if it acted as a white knight, we'd get to represent them if they pursued that course.

"In investment banking, ninety percent of the deals you propose are rejected by clients. They come to naught. Wasted effort, payless time. But when you have great information, when you know something's going to happen before the competition, your batting average soars. That's because you're not talking in the abstract. You're talking real world, real deals, things clients can chew on with their teeth. Things they can make money on. It's what everyone on Wall Street has always dreamed about. An honest-to-goodness-direct-from-the-Sears-catalogue crystal ball."

Did Levine's prescience raise eyebrows on Wall Street? At Lehman Brothers and subsequently at Drexel Burnham? Did the investment professionals responsible for his actions—some with decades of experience—question how and why this young upstart was so accurately wired into a kaleidoscope of market activities?

If so, their voices were mute. To hear it now, those who witnessed Levine's "extrasensory perception" first hand attributed it to nothing more sinister than a talent for tape-watching or a knack for courting the arbs. All perfectly legal but, as they well knew, all far from flawless. That Levine's knowledge was better than that of the other tape-watchers and arbs was reason to rejoice—and reason enough not to question how and where he got it. Apparently Dennis himself recognized this. By generating business for the firm—and by sharing the credit for his successes—he knew that he would divert attention from his methods to a myopic focus on what those methods produced.

"Dennis spent much of his time cold-calling prospective clients," says the Lehman colleague. "He'd ring up CEOs—they all come to the phone when you're with a major investment bank—and pitch ideas to them about acquiring this company, divesting [of] that one or serving as a white knight for another. He loved this, in part because it gave him access to corporate heavyweights. He'd then use that access to build relationships with Lehman's partners.

"For example, when a new business call clicked, when a CEO went for Dennis's pitch and agreed to sit down with the Lehman group, Dennis would give his superiors full credit for the break. Even when Dennis originated both the idea and the contact, he'd let his superiors call the client. Not that Dennis was Mr. Humble. He just knew—and he knew it instinctively—that to get ahead in investment banking you have to butter the egos of those in position to push you ahead.

"Dennis believed that two things motivate everyone on Wall Street. Greed and ego. And that's just what he appealed to. As long as he could make the partners look smarter than they were, and as long as he could make the firms richer than they were, no one would care how he learned what he learned or what else he did with it."

As long as he didn't get caught.

"The truth is there are a hundred men and women down here who are smarter than Dennis ever was because they're accomplishing what he didn't," says a prominent proxy solicitor. "They're committing the perfect crime. They're using inside information and they're getting away with it.

"The difference is that the really sharp operators aren't trading in stocks. They don't have secret accounts. They don't have dreams of making a billion dollars on the sly. Instead they have a system for making two million, three million, maybe five million a year—all in legitimate paychecks from the most respected investment banks.

"How do they do it? By cultivating sources—arbs, corporate counsels, PR guys, reporters, members of the merger bar—finding out about prospective deals while they're still just a gleam in a raider's eye, and then using this information to capture clients for the firm.

"Assume, for example, that investment banker Doe learns from merger lawyer Smith—whose law firm he has hired a dozen times and with whom, therefore, he has an IOU outstanding—that Steinberg is secretly stockpiling ABC Company stock and is thinking of launching a tender offer for the whole shooting match. Doe then takes this information to his firm, saying that he got it not from Smith, who is an insider, but instead from 'watching the tape.' Knowing that Doe's been on target in the past—his source is infinitely more accurate than tape-watching—his firm contacts ABC, warning of the Steinberg blitz and offering to help the target ward off the attack. Because Doe's firm alerted ABC to the imminent attack—because it proved it was on top of the market—it wins the client, finds a white knight, structures a friendly merger and collects a thirty-million-dollar fee, five hundred thousand of which winds up in Doe's bonus for serving as catalyst on the deal.

"And that's only the cake. For the icing, Doe is lauded as a psychic, a palm reader, a rainmaker, a superstar. That's what happened to Levine. It was one-half of his operation. If he'd stopped there, he'd have wound up on the cover of *Business Week*. Not as a criminal, but as a wunderkind."

In every way, the Lehman years were good for Levine. An M&A powerhouse laden with talented stars, the firm became a focal point of the explosive merger activity reshaping American industry in the early 1980s. With a roster of clients eager to tap its takeover expertise, there were more deals to do than people to do them. Recruiting—which drew new bodies in as fast as they could graduate from the law schools and MBA mills at Wharton, Harvard and Stanford—could barely keep up with the demand. For those on board, there were deals upon deals upon deals to be done. In this catch-as-catch-can environment, the learning curve was compressed into a short, high-speed arc. Before they were quite ready, trainees were doing the work of associates, associates were filling VP roles and the VPs, like Dennis Levine, were performing duties that in other circumstances would be padlocked by the partners. In the takeover era, the once slow and painstaking process of hand-tailoring a young man into an investment banker had been replaced with mass production.

"The lads who came into this business when I did were given a sense of history about their role in the world," says a senior Salomon Brothers partner. "We'd be assigned to work alongside an older man—one who'd been around long enough to see beyond the latest boom or bust and who could give the youngster a perspective on things. Most critical, he'd make the lad understand—my God, he'd say it a thousand times if he had to—that investment bankers owed their privileged position to trust. Without trust, we had nothing.

"It's painfully obvious to me that we haven't made that point to the current crop of youngsters. Maybe the pace has quickened so that no one—Lord, I hate to admit—has taken the time. Or maybe no one cares. In either case, that's a terrible shame."

What the voice from the past fails to understand is that Dennis Levine and his peers gravitated toward the investment banks precisely because the traditional grooming process gave way to a career track devoid of ethics or history or any such thing that didn't translate into dollars. In promising more and faster money than any other profession, in sneering at the law firms with whom they compete for top grads as plodding institutions, the investment banks sent an engraved invitation to all those seeking a shortcut to the top.

Dennis Levine discovered just how fast the track could be—
and how it never seemed fast enough. Turning thirty during his
first year at Lehman, he looked in the mirror to find he'd become
the investment banker he had Walter Mittyed about since his
Baruch days. But he wanted more. Millions more. As much
money as the clients he served. As much money as Wall Street
could offer.

And he set out to get it. With each deal, with each increment
of responsibility and experience, Levine widened his web of Wall
Street contacts, massaging the arbs, courting the lawyers, brown-
ing the clients. Through it all, he was busy on three fronts, for-
tifying his position at Lehman, pruning the underground
grapevine he'd first planted while at Smith Barney, and using
both to compound his gains at Bank Leu, where he'd become the
institution's biggest brokerage customer. By December 1983 his
inside trading profits, all neatly tucked away in the seemingly
safe and secret Bahamas, totaled more than $3,000,000.

To the Queens boy turned East Side burgher, this success vin-
dicated what he had long come to believe. That if he put his
mind to it—if he effectively camouflaged his actions—he could
fool all of the people all of the time. His dream, to make $100
million by age thirty-five, now seemed within reach and it was
proving easier than he had ever believed. And more fun too.

"When I was a kid I went through a period where I was the
terror of Woolworth's," says a proxy solicitor who worked with
Levine on two deals. "I mean, I'd steal everything that wasn't
tied down. Baseball cards, Spaldings, Baby Ruths, Cracker
Jacks, plastic Thunderbirds. For about a year—I think it was in
the sixth grade—the greatest fun, the greatest thrill I had was
shoplifting. The fact that I could do it at will and get away with
it—well, that just seemed incredible. So I did it again and again
and again. Only after I got caught walking out of Smolkoff's
candy store with a kite stuffed down the leg of my chinos did I
stop. Until that point, it was heart-pounding joy. And I would bet
that for Dennis Levine—seeing that he too could get away with

it—it was the most fun he had with or without his clothes on. The more he did it—and the more he could get away with what he was doing—the more he couldn't stop."

But his biggest scores—and his ultimate fall—were yet to come.

IV

The French Connection

"I shouldn't spend my nights worrying about a corporate raider. I should be worrying about how to make better cars."
—ROBERT S. MILLER, *vice-chairman of the Chrysler Corporation, quoted in* The New York Times, *November 3, 1986*

It was, on the surface, a routine M&A transaction. David Arledge, chief financial officer for The Coastal Corporation, informed Drexel Burnham Lambert, which had recently hired Dennis Levine from Lehman Brothers, of its interest in making a tender offer for American Natural Resources (ANR). Within weeks Levine, who had been asked by Drexel managing director John Sorte to work on the deal, learned of ANR's identity as a takeover candidate and promptly passed the information on to Ivan Boesky, with whom he had negotiated a profit-sharing relationship.

Under the terms of the unusual, and highly illegal, arrangement Levine would relay inside information in return for 1 to 5 percent of Boesky's profits. (The lower figure applied to those stocks Boesky already owned, but in which he increased his position as a result of Levine's tip. Thus Levine hoped to gain twice: both on his own 145,500-share purchase of ANR and on Boesky's stake.

Well before the deal was consummated, both men sat with invaluable knowledge of the pending takeover. But they were not alone. Although headlines of the Levine–Boesky case have focused attention on the cast of principal insiders, many others routinely learn of secret transactions just as early. Most are supporting players—including lawyers, broker/dealers, proxy solicitors, accountants, consultants or bankers—who are asked to review the deals with an eye toward participating in them as legal or business professionals.

This "legal leakage" is so extensive as to render any effort at secrecy into little more than a foolish charade. Thus the absurdity of the insider trading laws: while Levine could not legally divulge news of the deal to Boesky, because there was no legitimate business purpose for doing so, Coastal could get on the hotline, spreading word to a long list of outsiders—all without breaking the law.

The full extent of this predeal leak is revealed in testimony Arledge gave to the SEC:

> *SEC:* "Coastal began to consider ANR as an attractive takeover possibility. Is that correct?"
>
> *Arledge:* "That is correct."
>
> *SEC:* "Did Coastal disclose to Bankers Trust its interest in possibly acquiring ANR?"
>
> *Arledge:* "Yes."
>
> *SEC:* "What role did Bankers Trust play in the ANR acquisition?
>
> *Arledge:* "It was one of the two agent banks in arranging financing."
>
> *SEC:* "What do you mean by an 'agent bank'?"
>
> *Arledge:* "There are the two—one of two banks that was engaged to form a syndicate of banks to provide bank funds for the financing to acquire American Natural Resources. . . ."
>
> *SEC:* "And you contacted a lot of people in that effort, didn't you?"
>
> *Arledge:* "Yes."
>
> *SEC:* "In addition to Bankers Trust, you contacted Citibank. Isn't that correct?"
>
> *Arledge:* "Yes."
>
> *SEC:* "Citibank was also an agent bank in this transaction?"
>
> *Arledge:* "Yes."
>
> *SEC:* "In mid-January you contacted Skadden Arps. Is that correct?"
>
> *Arledge:* "Yes."

SEC: "And you retained Skadden Arps as counsel to Coastal in connection with this acquisition. Correct?"

Arledge: "Yes."

SEC: "Skadden was retained because you believed they had particular expertise in mergers and acquisitions. Is that correct?"

Arledge: "Yes. . . ."

SEC: "During the same period, you also talked with a group called Stock Management, Inc. Is that correct?"

Arledge: "Yes."

SEC: "Who were they?"

Arledge: "It was also our consultants in New York."

SEC: "And you told them that ANR was a possible target. Correct?"

Arledge: "Yes."

SEC: "You also had contacts in January 1985 with the law firm of Cahill Gordon. Correct?"

Arledge: "Correct."

SEC: "And what was Cahill Gordon's role in this possible acquisition?"

Arledge: "Cahill Gordon represented Drexel Burnham. . . ."

SEC: "During the week including January 22 to January 25, 1985, Cahill Gordon learned that ANR was a possible acquisition candidate, if it didn't know before. Isn't that correct?"

Arledge: "Correct."

SEC: "And during same week, the law firm of White and Case also learned, if it didn't know before, that ANR was a possible acquisition candidate. Correct?"

Arledge: "Yes."

SEC: "Now, what role did White and Case play here?"

Arledge: "They represented the agent banks, particularly Bankers Trust."

SEC: "Now, also in January of 1985, you and other representatives of Coastal had contacts with the National Commercial Bank of Saudi Arabia. Isn't that correct?"

Arledge: "Yes."

SEC: "You talked to these Saudi Arabian bankers in order to arrange possible financing for the ANR transaction. Correct?"

Arledge: "Correct."

SEC: "You yourself took a trip to Saudi Arabia. You were there on February 5, 1985. Correct?"

Arledge: "Yes."

SEC: "And you met with representatives of the National Commercial Bank of Saudi Arabia on that visit. Correct?"

Arledge: "Correct."

SEC: "How many people did you meet with there, representing the Saudi Arabian bank?"

Arledge: "Approximately four. . . ."

SEC: "And you told these representatives of the Saudi Arabian bank that ANR was a possible acquisition candidate. Correct?"

Arledge: "They were aware."

SEC: "How did they become aware?"

Arledge: "I previously had met with certain representatives of that institution in Geneva, Switzerland."

SEC: "Were there representatives of other institutions at the Geneva meeting?"

Arledge: "No."

SEC: "Now, the Saudis retained the law firm of Baker and Botts to represent them. Is that correct?"

Arledge: "Yes."

SEC: "And by no later than February 3, 1985, Baker and Botts also knew that ANR was a possible takeover candidate. Correct?"

Arledge: "Yes."

SEC: "You met with another Arab bank on February 6, 1985, in London. Is that correct?"

Arledge: "Yes."

SEC: "That is the Arab Banking Corporation."

Arledge: "Yes. . . ."

SEC: "Now, you also met in London on the sixth with Orion Royal Limited. Is that correct?"

Arledge: "Yes."

SEC: "Is that an English bank?"

Arledge: "Yes it is."

SEC: "And they learned that you were interested in possibly acquiring ANR. Is that correct?"

Arledge: "I don't think we ever identified to Orion the name of ANR."

SEC: "Now, during the period of February 8 to February 14, 1985, you had meetings with representatives of several banks in Houston, didn't you?"

Arledge: "Yes."

SEC: "One of those banks was the Toronto Dominion Bank of Canada?"

Arledge: "Yes."

SEC: "And you told Toronto Dominion that ANR was a possible takeover candidate. Correct?"

Arledge: "Sometime during this period, we disclosed the name of ANR. Yes. . . ."

SEC: "You also told the Royal Bank of Canada during that period that ANR was a possible acquisition target. Correct?"

Arledge: "Yes."

SEC: "You told the same information to Canadian Imperial Bank."

Arledge: "Yes."

SEC: "And to Bank of Montreal."

Arledge: "Yes."

And on and on . . .

While Wall Street's investment banks are viewed as the major conduits of inside information, the commercial banks are also in the inner circle, as Arledge's testimony reveals, and they learn of a stream of deals before they are made public. Because raiders must assemble a package of financing to acquire target companies, the banks find themselves being asked to review and support pending bids before they are made public.

Just how this works is illustrated by the inner workings of a new and interesting player in the M&A field, France's Banque Paribas.

Drawn to mergers and acquisitions by the same big-dollar lure that has proved irresistible to arbs, investment bankers, lawyers and takeover artists, Paribas has carved out a niche as a loyal ally of the corporate raiders. In bankrolling the sharks, Paribas—which has only 150 employees in New York—has become Wall Street's version of the mouse that roared. Tending its U.S. acquisition financing business is the Franco-American duet of vice-presidents Bernard Allorent and Joseph Francht, Jr.

The New York office of Paribas entered the U.S. market in the late seventies as a standard retail banking and lending outpost for its Paris-based parent, and for years the branch was just another bit player in Manhattan's highly competitive financial community. But that wouldn't last long. Soon enough, changes in the banking industry would force Paribas to revise its marketing strategy.

With traditional corporate lending on the skids and ever larger numbers of large companies turning to more creative financing, including junk bonds, to fulfill their capital needs, banks were pressed to find new ways of making money. Casting an envious eye on the likes of Drexel Burnham and First Boston, many put new emphasis on their own investment banking arms, hired Wall Street stars and generally beefed up their deal-making capabilities.

Smitten with Wall Street in its own right—and eager to participate in the wholesale restructurings changing the face of American business—Allorent hit upon a related strategy for Paribas. The French-owned bank would cultivate a niche as lender to the corporate raiders, thus filling a void in the capital markets.

Paribas knew that in spite of the money-center banks' multi-billion-dollar commitment to the M&A business, independent raiders seeking to finance hostile deals could find themselves strapped for adequate funds to acquire the target's stock. You could blame it on conservative banking policies and on defensive strategies designed to block the sharks from feeding on their prey. Knowing that the big banks were reluctant to finance raids against established customers, many corporations fearful of takeovers initiated a series of banking relationships for the sole purpose of tying up banks that might otherwise line up against them.

So when the raider shopped for money, he might find that Manny Hanny, Citibank, Chase and Bankers Trust were already spoken for. Other banks, though free of conflicting relationships, might also turn thumbs down to the deal, preferring to steer clear of hostile deals as a matter of policy.

"The big banks are afraid of their shadows," says a partner with a New York–based Big Eight accounting firm. "Some that could do a land-office business in takeovers stay away for fear of alienating the corporate establishment. The thinking goes like this: if we make our beds with the entrepreneurs who are picking off the nation's CEOs like ducks at a shooting gallery, what will happen when the merger craze cools off? Then we'll have burned our bridges behind us. The raiders will be gone and the chief executives—who'd then view us as turncoats—would refuse to do business with us!

"That's the nightmare that keeps some of the banks about a mile away from unfriendly takeovers. But fear isn't the only thing that holds them back. Even those big banks with the balls to back the nastiest bidders find that they can't deliver as promised. Because they're so clumsy and bureaucratic—and because they don't really feel comfortable evaluating takeovers from a credit standpoint—they move too slowly to play the raider's game. He needs straight, fast, shoot-from-the-hip answers but winds up instead with the runaround."

"Paribas stepped into this crazy quilt of ifs, ands and maybes with a simple declarative message that had to warm the hearts of the raider community. In effect it said: "We don't care who you are or who it is you're after, if the deal is good we'll finance it."

Getting its feet wet as a participating player in loans syndicated by other banks, Paribas quickly aspired to a more pivotal role, that of the lead bank in takeover deals. Acting in this capacity, the lead bank commits to raising all or part of a shark's war chest, ponying up some of the money itself and then enlisting a syndicate of banks to provide the balance. Because the lead banker serves as point man for the syndicate, because he alone commits to raising the money, he is the first to have contact with the raider and thus to learn of a pending transaction.

At what point does the lead bank join the takeover team? When does it learn of the raider's "secret" battle plan, and what does it do with that information? Is it locked in the bank's vaults or spread further along the Wall Street rumor mill?

To get some answers, one needs to explore Paribas's first major deal as a lead bank.

The events began in February 1986, when New York–based MacFadden Publications asked Dan Good, then E. F. Hutton's M&A chief, to look for attractive acquisition candidates in a related business. Although Wall Street's infatuation with media outfits had pushed their stock prices into the ionosphere, Mac-Fadden hoped to find a media company whose shares had for one reason or another not yet taken off like a Roman candle. Call it a search for hidden values—a quest common among corporate raiders.

After intensive research in the media business, Hutton proposed a Christmas list of takeover candidates, all of which Mac-Fadden chairman Peter Callahan promptly rejected as overpriced, overrated or simply uninteresting. Digging deeper, Hutton then identified a new set of prospects, including one— John Blair & Company—that MacFadden saw as a diamond in the rough. A sluggish performer saddled with money-losing divisions, Blair was primed for a drastic pruning that MacFadden knew would quickly restore the bottom line. To Callahan it was a healthy company buried inside a sick one. Nothing a little corporate surgery wouldn't cure.

MacFadden secretly began acquiring the company's stock on

the open market, accumulating 4.9 percent of Blair's outstanding shares—enough to gain a grubstake in the company without crossing the 5-percent threshold that forces the buyer to notify the SEC (through a so-called 13-D filing), and in turn the public, of its holdings.

By keeping the takeover secret until a full-blown tender offer was announced, MacFadden, like other raiders, hoped to prevent a stampede for the target's shares, which would inflate its price and make the company far more costly to acquire. But in this environment absolute secrecy is impossible. Even the most independent shark—a sole entrepreneur who for most of his business dealings acts as a committee of one—must discuss his plans with outsiders before the tender is launched. He needs legal guidance (does the target have "built-in defenses"?), a proxy firm (to tender the shares) and financing allies (to bankroll the deal). It is in this prefiling period that the raider informs these professional insiders of his plan to acquire the target. Under cover of secrecy, the "incestuous cast of characters" learns what the public will not know for days, weeks or months to come.

It was in this "confidential" stage that MacFadden, having decided to launch a full-scale tender offer for Blair, asked Dan Good to help arrange the necessary financing. Knowing that Paribas was receptive to this type of deal—and that it was eager to make a name for itself in the takeover market—Good asked the bankers to meet with the takeover team at Hutton's New York offices.

Putting his cards on the table, Callahan revealed his financing strategy. To be named lead bank, Paribas would have to commit to more than a third of the $300 million it would take to acquire Blair's common stock. The balance would come from MacFadden's own funds and junk bonds to be issued by Hutton.

Sensing the opportunity to play a key role in a major transaction, Paribas executives were inclined to flash the green light even though they had little experience in lending to media companies. After reviewing the deal for less than two weeks, Paribas inked a commitment letter, agreeing to raise the capital on a best-efforts basis. The next day MacFadden proceeded with its tender offer.

Clearly, the Paribas people were privy to valuable inside information soon after they were introduced to MacFadden. But the road would not end there. Once the senior bankers decided to pursue MacFadden's request, it became necessary to inform others in the chain of command about the secret deal.

As the bank's decision-making machinery went into action, word spread across an intercontinental hotline that started in New York and moved quickly to Paris. Conforming with internal procedures at Paribas, the proposal to make the loan was relayed first to Direction de l'Amerique, a Paris-based credit liaison which serves as an intermediary between the New York outpost and the bank's central committee.

Through this process, news of the deal reached about half a dozen individuals at Direction de l'Amerique and about the same number at the central committee. By the time the bank made its ultimate decision it was likely that twenty or more principals, plus their staff members (and, if there was abuse, their friends and relatives), had learned of the "secret" takeover. Add to this the investment bankers, proxy solicitors and the lawyers also informed at this time; and the core of insiders—including professionals, secretaries, clerks and assorted assistants—could easily have topped fifty or more. Were they to have shared what they knew (à la Levine, Tome and Thayer) with accomplices, professional investors, relatives, friends, taxicab drivers and elevator operators, all of whom would have in turn told their friends, lovers, mistresses and brothers-in-law, the insider pool could have grown to hundreds—all able to purchase securities with advance knowledge unavailable to the general market.

While there is no evidence that Banque Paribas executives trade on the basis of this information—and all insist that they do not—there is no doubt that the bank relies on a flimsy system of controls, mostly faith in the employees' honesty, to prevent it. But as Dennis Levine found at Smith Barney, at Lehman Brothers and ultimately at Drexel Burnham, blind faith in an employee's honesty creates an environment in which the inside trader can thrive. In effect, the trusting employee (or, as in the Tome case, trusting friend) becomes the inside trader's greatest ally.

Like most of the other players in the takeover business, Paribas clings to trust in its people—and a faith in their professionalism—as its major defense against insider trading. So much so that it sees no reason to produce a written code of conduct for bank employees.

"The law's the law," Francht says. "Everybody understands the law. For an institution to come out and say 'Here's the law,' I think, is unnecessary when you're dealing with a small group of professionals."

There is truth in what Francht says. Throughout his career, Levine signed document after document, swearing on a stack of Bibles that he had no secret securities accounts, that he would never reveal inside information, much less trade on it, and that underneath his banker's pinstripes was a Boy Scout uniform. The truth is that M&A professionals know the rules on confidentiality so well they could spell them backward. Those inclined to violate them will do so, whether they are reminded of the law or not. The only effective defense against insider trading is to make the penalties so harsh that those tempted to violate the law will think the punishment too great to merit the risk.

"You know the old saw: 'If you can't do the time, don't do the crime,'" says a Wall Street investor who operates his own arbitrage business. "Well, most of the people who engage in insider trading are white-collar types who turn pale at the thought of an hour in jail. Were they to be convinced that inside traders get the same treatment as convicted car thieves—in other words, a couple of Christmases behind bars—most would keep their hands out of the till no matter how great the temptation.

"That's why the fate of Levine and Boesky and company is so critical. Should those two walk away from their roles in the greatest scandal in Wall Street's history with little more than an F on their report cards, well, that's not going to discourage others from going down the same road. They'll look at a Boesky and say, 'He started free and rich and he ended free and rich, so why not try what he did?'

"But if Levine and Boesky go to jail—and if *The New York Times* runs a front-page picture of them being led away in hand-cuffs, well, then you have the best defense you can ever have against inside trading. Nothing else will work."

V

Old School Ties

"Certain guys, you put them in a room with streetfighters and they're streetfighters. Put them in a room with genteel WASPs and they're WASPs. Dennis could be both. He could be whatever he had to be to manipulate people. To win them over. To gain their confidence and get them to like him.

"Underneath it all was a desire to succeed. To make it in investment banking and to get rich. For Dennis it was a blinding obsession."

To the question: "Isn't getting rich the universal goal of investment bankers?" the reply is:

"There are guys who want to be rich and there are guys who want to be RICH.

—A former Lehman Brothers colleague on Dennis Levine

onvinced that the SEC was nothing more than a paper tiger and that its brain-dead bureaucrats would never find him, much less arrest him, Levine pressed the accelerator to the floor, stepping up the pace and the stakes of his inside trading juggernaut.

From autumn 1982 to November 1984, while still at Lehman Brothers, Levine fed his habit twenty-two times, netting profits of roughly $5 million. Major scores included the following:

- Maryland Cup Corporation's merger with the Fort Howard Paper Company. Levine, who learned of the pending transaction when Maryland Cup hired Lehman in June 1983, purchased 15,200 shares of the client's stock at an average price of $39.26 per share. Bank Leu portfolio manager Bernhard Meier, now routinely piggybacking on his client's prescient stock picks, purchased 300 shares for his own account. In June 1983, when Fort Howard and Maryland Cup publicly announced their agreement, whereby Fort Howard would purchase Maryland Cup at $52 a share, the stock soared. On July 7, Levine cashed in his chips for a profit of $121,807; Meier, not yet a true believer, settled for $1,769.

- In the fall of 1983, Esquire Corporation retained Lehman for investment banking advice on its proposed acquisition by Gulf & Western Industries. From October 28 to November 21, Levine purchased (presumably from his favorite Wall Street phone booth) 15,000 shares of Esquire common at an average price of $15.26 a share. Meier followed the lead, again buying 300 shares (average price $17.77 each). The good news came on December 5, when Gulf & Western announced it would acquire Esquire for $25 a share. With the stock rising immediately, Levine dumped all of his Esquire holdings between December 5 and December 8 at an average sale price of $23.37 per share, for a profit of $121,728. Meier, still peeling potatoes, pocketed $1,680.

· While the Gulf & Western deal was unfolding, Levine was active on another front. When Cone Mills learned on November 9 that it was targeted for a hostile takeover by Western Pacific Industries, it turned to Lehman to help structure a leveraged buyout. Knowing that the deal would propel Cone's stock to new highs, Levine got on the Bahamas hotline, ordering about 20,000 Cone shares at an average price of $61.76 each. Two weeks later he took his reward, collecting profits of $83,680 on per-share prices of about $65.94.

· In early 1984 Levine made his biggest score to date. Learning in early March that the Jewel Companies would be subject to a tender offer by Lehman's client American Stores, he started buying the stock, gradually adding to his position through the spring until his Bank Leu portfolio held 75,000 shares (average price: $49.45 per share). Touting the stock to Meier, Levine hinted that a takeover was in the making and that a little patience would be well rewarded. Truer words were never spoken. On June 1, American Stores went public with a $70 per-share tender offer for Jewel stock. Within a week, Levine cashed in his Jewel chips at an average price of $65.54 each, collecting a profit of $1,206,275.

With his stock picks hitting so accurately, and with his Bank Leu account swelling ever larger for it, Levine took great pains to keep his bankers as plump and buttered as Thanksgiving turkeys. A true believer in human greed, he knew that the best way to turn a potential whistleblower into an accomplice is to grease his palms. Levine encouraged Bernhard Meier, who in turn encouraged Bruno Pletscher, to trade along with him. By spreading the addiction to insider trading and by making the others accomplices in his plot, Levine was certain that these otherwise perfect strangers would work like brothers to keep his activities and his identity secret.

Just how Levine clued in his cohorts came to light years later in Pletscher's secret testimony to the SEC.

SEC: "Did Mr. Meier make any statements to you about expecting an increase in the price of Jewel at the time that he recommended this [the Jewel stock] to you for the second time?"

Pletscher: "Mr. Meier . . . got information from Mr. X referring to Jewel. I cannot remember what was said, but I remember I said I have so much Jewel and I did not like the idea of being invested in stocks for a long period of time. He said [to] be patient; the information he has is something is going to happen, but it takes a little more time."

SEC: "That was information which he said he got from Mr. X?"

Pletscher: "That is what he told me, yes."

SEC: "Did you make a profit on your investment in Jewel?"

Pletscher: "Yes, I did."

SEC: "Did you recall whether there was some public announcement or event which caused the price to increase?"

Pletscher: "Prior to the event I was told a takeover situation is going to take place, but I cannot recall whether or not it really took place."

SEC: "Who told you that?"

Pletscher: "Mr. Meier."

SEC: "Did he attribute that statement to Mr. X?"
Pletscher: "Yes, he did."

While Levine counseled Meier in the virtues of patience, he may have acted personally to speed up the deal. Buying Jewel stock soon after American Stores approached Lehman Brothers about a possible takeover, Levine expected to turn a fast profit on the deal. Waiting wasn't part of his game plan. In deal after deal, he had bought, sold and banked his gain in about the time it takes a New York check to clear in Los Angeles. When Clabir Corporation tendered for HMW Industries, the announcement came two days after Dennis bought his stake. With RCA stock it took three days, three again for Instrumentation Laboratory and about a week for Alexander & Alexander Services.

But weeks after the initial Jewel purchases, the deal appeared to be in jeopardy. For a man accustomed to risk-free investing, this was cause for panic. Determined to move things along, some of Levine's former colleagues now believe that the inside trader in their midst started rumors about Jewel in order to protect his position in the stock.

"After our initial discussions with American Stores concerning a tender offer for Jewel, the client lay back, doing nothing for months," says a onetime Lehmanite, now with another investment bank. "But then rumors started flying that Jewel would be the subject of a leveraged buyout. With the stock rising on the news, American Stores—which didn't want to pay any more for the stock than it had to—got off its rump and went for Jewel. There's a feeling that Dennis started those rumors in order to get the deal done and to get his money out of the Jewel stock."

Levine abused his role as an investment banker in many ways, but perhaps never so glaringly as in his drive to cultivate a ring of inside traders. The relationship with his first accomplice, Robert Wilkis, dated back to the Citibank days. Wilkis had been secretly trading for his own accounts since 1980, the same year Levine opened his secret Nassau account. Moving on to Lazard Frères in 1981, Wilkis continued his activities, buying and selling stocks through clandestine accounts at Credit Suisse (Bahamas) Limited, the Bank of Nova Scotia Trust Company (Cayman Islands branch) and Guinness Mahon Bank Limited (also in the Cayman Islands).

At some point early in their careers, Levine and Wilkis agreed to a buddy system whereby the two would share their investment banking intelligence and use the scoop they learned from each other to trade in securities, mostly those of takeover stocks. Using the code name Alan Darby, Wilkis alerted Levine, whose code name was Mike Schwartz, to at least nineteen such opportunities.

How the men communicated is still a mystery, but upon piecing together what is known of their modus operandi from interviews with friends and business associates, one might suspect that Wilkis telephoned Levine at work, using his code name, and that Levine called Wilkis at home to get the scoop on, for example, The Limited's move to buy out Carter Hawley Hale Stores.

Hearing from Wilkis that he was in for 20,000 shares, Levine was soon—from March 24 to March 27—on the walkie-talkie to Bank Leu to purchase 34,000 shares of Carter Hawley Hale Stores. On April 2 The Limited's tender offer hit the Dow Jones wire, sending the stock upward. By April 5 Levine sold his shares for a gain of $222,148; Wilkis turned his 20,000 shares into a profit of $95,000, and Meier settled for $6,729.

But Wilkis was not Levine's only informant. By the time of The Limited deal, he had already established an illicit relationship with former Smith Barney buddy and now Lehman Brothers colleague Ira Sokolow. Sokolow, a thirty-two-year-old vice-president at Lehman with degrees from Harvard and Wharton, was earning a perhaps inadequate annual salary of $400,000; he would be paid cash for his tips. Levine would soon build ties to Ilan Reich, a thirty-one-year-old Wachtell, Lipton law partner who earned $500,000 a year; Reich would pass him information on client activities. Extending the underground network even further, Sokolow hammered out a cash-for-leaks deal with Goldman Sachs banker David Brown, also thirty-one, and bearing paper from prestigious Wharton. Thus was born Wall Street's version of the bucket brigade.

Just how the system worked is illustrated by Brown's first inside tip, word of a proposed leveraged buyout of McGraw-Edison. Acting on the leak, Levine purchased 79,500 McGraw-Edison shares, selling out a week later for a profit of $906,836. Meier, piggybacking on his favorite customer, earned $12,750 on a sale of 1,000 shares. Pletscher, piggybacking on Meier, added to his personal account. Sokolow, who would ultimately earn $120,000 for a bushel basket full of tips, was paid a token fee by Levine and shared the proceeds with Brown. For Brown this was the first installment of $30,000 in illegal payoffs that would wreck a promising investment banking career that would likely have generated $20 million in lifetime earnings.

SEC: "You invested in McGraw-Edison?"

Pletscher: "Yes."

SEC: "Was that a stock which you were told Mr. X was investing in?"

Pletscher: "I was told that Mr. X has invested in McGraw-Edison."

SEC: "Did Mr. Meier tell you that?"

Pletscher: "Yes, he did."

SEC: "What else, if anything, did Mr. Meier tell you about McGraw-Edison or about what Mr. X had said about McGraw-Edison?"

Pletscher: "In respect to McGraw-Edison I got information from Mr. Meier that this is a takeover situation which will take place soon. . . ."

SEC: "Did Mr. Meier indicate that Mr. X had told him, Mr. Meier, that McGraw-Edison was a situation where a takeover would take place?"

Pletscher: "As a general remark I can say that whenever I got an information from Mr. Meier pointing out a takeover situation, this was referring to Mr. X. To the best of my recollection, I cannot recall any event where Mr.

Meier mentioned a takeover situation without having Mr. X involved in a trade."

SEC: "Do you remember anything else that Mr. Meier said about McGraw-Edison when he recommended the investment in McGraw-Edison?"

Pletscher: "To the best of my recollection, he said, 'This is a sure winner.'"

SEC: "Was Mr. Meier right? Did you make a profit in McGraw-Edison?"

Pletscher: "Yes, I made a nice profit."

Just as he had dreamed from the first days of his career, Levine sat at the center of a Wall Street switchboard that flashed status reports on dozens of companies engaged in sensitive and supposedly secret negotiations with lawyers and investment bankers. That he could conceive of a clandestine trading ring with tentacles extending throughout the financial community is not at all surprising. Given their unlimited access to confidential information and their intimate knowledge of the price tag that information carries, hundreds of Wall Street professionals have had similar if not identical dreams. But what made Levine's scheme so exceptional was that it turned from fantasy to reality and that it succeeded in attracting bright young men into its fold. Wilkis, Sokolow, Brown and Reich were solid members of Wall Street's junior establishment, earning handsome salaries of up to half a million dollars a year and climbing faster than a hot penny stock.

"Wall Street, Main Street, Las Vegas, wherever—there have always been men like Dennis Levine and Robert Wilkis," says a Wall Street commodities broker. "Call them gamblers. For everything in life they figure the risks, calculate the odds of making it work and estimate the payoffs should their numbers come in. That's how they decide on marriage, parenthood, friendship and career. Weigh the odds, evaluate the risks, project the returns. Day-to-day decision making.

"But then one morning they wake up to find a real honey. A once-in-a-lifetime chance to break the bank, or, if they fail, to go stone-broke in the process. They ponder it for awhile, but because the prospective payoff is so staggering—so clearly the stuff of dreams—they can't resist. They pay their money and take their chances.

"You can understand these men. They accept the classic risk/reward trade-off. But what you can't understand are the dummies who put up a million to win five dollars. Like the guys who risked their careers to make a few thousand bucks with Dennis Levine. They accepted killer odds to make dime-store gains. To me, they're certified shmucks."

That all were willing to break the law, violate their professional ethics and in the process risk all that they had achieved indicates the depths of greed that fouls the Wall Street of the eighties. And it reveals the arrogance of the Street's young superachievers, convinced of being too smart, too sly to fail at anything. Inside trading was just another opportunity to prove how smart and sly they were—that they could, as Dennis Levine believed, outfox the system.

Levine would put this belief to the test in October 1984, when his inside trading ring had its first brush with disaster. It all began when Wilkis's firm, Lazard Frères, was retained by Chicago Pacific Corporation to draft a battle plan for a hostile takeover of Textron. With a window of opportunity before the tender offer would be publicly announced, Wilkis, who purchased 29,000 shares of Textron stock through the Bank of Nova Scotia Trust Company's Cayman Island branch, informed Levine of the pending deal. Acting on this tip, Levine ordered 51,500 Textron shares for his Bank Leu portfolio.

When Chicago Pacific's cash offer hit the Dow Jones wire near the end of October, the stock rose dramatically, enabling Wilkis and Levine to bail out for profits of $100,000 and $200,000, respectively.

Easy as pie. But not quite. In a routine computer scan of market activity, the SEC detected a disturbing spurt in the price and volume of Textron shares just before news of the tender offer was made public. While these preannouncement run-ups are as common as IBM dividends—proof positive that inside trading is standard operating procedure on Wall Street—the SEC targets the more glaring cases for further investigation. In reviewing the Textron case, the Feds learned from the company's management that Dennis Levine, an investment banker with Lehman Brothers, had called the company before the tender offer was announced, indicating that Textron would be the target of a hostile takeover. By tipping the executives to a pending crisis, Levine hoped to win the company as a Lehman client. While this is a standard investment banking ploy, the SEC had no idea Levine had traded in Textron or any other stock, and wanted to know how the Lehman VP knew Textron was a target before the takeover was announced.

Subpoenaed by the Feds to answer this and other questions, Levine arrived at the SEC's offices at 1 Battery Park Plaza on November 14, 1984, as cool as an arb holding the perfect hedge.

With a straight face, Levine claimed he had heard of the Textron play from two men talking in Drexel Burnham's offices, that he had no securities brokerage accounts, that he had no discretionary trading authority over any securities brokerage accounts and that from April 1 to November 14 of that year he had not transacted in any securities of Textron. Levine's statements reveal a well-rehearsed and carefully concocted story to cover up his clandestine activities and provide rare insight into his modus operandi as an investment banker. Through his testimony we see the extent to which the most prestigious firms will scavenge for business.

SEC: "Would you state your full name including your middle name, Mr. Levine."
Levine: "Dennis Levine."
SEC: "Have you ever used any other names?"
Levine: "No."

This was an outright lie. By this time he had already used the code names Mr. Diamond and Mike Schwartz.

SEC: "Do you have discretionary trading authority over any securities brokerage accounts?"

Levine: "No. . . ."

SEC: "Within the last year have you become involved in consideration or work directed at a possible offer to acquire a company called Textron, Inc.?"

Levine: "Can you repeat the question, please?"

SEC: "Within the last year have you become involved, in connection with your work, with consideration of a possible offer for Textron, Inc.? I mean consideration in the broadest sense—analysis, even if it is not for a client."

Levine: "I just don't understand what is meant by 'consideration,' I'm sorry."

Clearly, Levine is a tough nut to crack. Not only has he lied about his brokerage accounts, he has also gone hard of hearing and feigned illiteracy.

SEC: "Have you had an occasion in the last year to analyze Textron?"

Levine: "Yes."

SEC: "When was the first occasion within the last year you had to analyze Textron?"

Levine: "In October 1984."

SEC: "And how did it come to occur in October 1984 that you began analyzing Textron?"

Levine: "Pursuant to a rumor that Textron may be the subject of an unsolicited offer. As investment bankers we thought it incumbent on us to analyze Textron's vulnerability to an unsolicited offer, bring the rumor of such an unsolicited offer to the attention of Textron and attempt to have Textron retain Lehman Brothers as its financial adviser."

SEC: "When did you first become aware of this rumor?"

Levine: "First week of October."

SEC: "Do you remember which day it was during that week?"

Levine: "Not specifically."

SEC: "How did you become aware of this rumor?"

Levine: "I was in the reception area of Drexel Burnham in New York and overheard a conversation between two gentlemen."

SEC: "Do you know who these gentlemen were?"

Levine: "No, I don't."

SEC: "What was it that you overheard these two gentlemen say?"

Levine: "I will describe for you the conversation I overheard. One gentleman was talking to the other and discussed the following: Lester Crown has a group together with approximately $300 million equity and they need an additional billion-plus dollars to accomplish their objective. That although the economics of the transaction are attractive, Bankers Trust could be a problem and we should consider these guys and Citibank as alternates.

"I then overheard what I would characterize as garbled, where they said something about a 13-D filing, the words 'Skadden Arps' and 'First Boston,' and also 'fireworks in Rhode Island,' which is a direct quote."

SEC: "How is it that you relate this conversation to Textron?"

Levine: "By piecing together the operative statement that there would be 'fireworks in Rhode Island' and a transaction in excess of a million dollars, I deduced that what they were probably talking about was Textron as a target."

SEC: "What information led you to deduce that they were probably talking about Textron?"

Levine: "The indicated size of the financing required, the fact that Rhode Island was a place where there would be some fireworks."

SEC: "Prior to this occasion did you have some general

knowledge of Textron, some general familiarity with Textron?"

Levine: "General familiarity, yes."

SEC: "Were there any particular reasons for you having this general familiarity with Textron?"

Levine: "Having been in this business for as many years as me, you learn a lot about different companies and who acquirers are and who potential targets are, and Textron is always a name that generally comes up as somebody both acquisition-oriented and rumored to have been a takeover target themselves."

SEC: "Did you mention these rumors to anyone at Lehman Brothers?"

Levine: "Yes."

SEC: "And to whom did you mention this?"

Levine: "Steve Waters."

SEC: "What is Mr. Waters's position?"

Levine: "Steve Waters is a managing director at Lehman Brothers."

SEC: "When did you mention it to him?"

Levine: "A few days later."

SEC: "What did you tell him when you mentioned this rumor to him?"

Levine: "I told Mr. Waters that I had heard a rumor that Textron may be the subject of an unsolicited offer and that we should call the company and inform them of this rumor and see if we can position the firm to be retained by Textron should this materialize."

SEC: "And did you indicate to Mr. Waters how it was that you came to hear this rumor?"

Levine: "No."

SEC: "What response, if any, did he have when you told him about the rumor?"

Levine: "'Let's call the company.'"

SEC: "Was there some reason why you did not tell Mr. Waters or anyone else at Lehman the day that you heard the rumor?"

Levine: "Yes. When I originally overheard this conversation, they did mention a 13-D filing. I assumed that there was some kind of a buyout program. However, when I went back to my office and I looked at Textron stocks, it did not appear to be trading in any unusual manner at all. However, on my Quotron screen I did put the symbol for Textron up so I could continue to monitor it, and on the day . . . I saw the stock trading up one point in a down market on heavier-than-normal volume, I brought it to the attention of Mr. Waters and on that basis we placed our phone call to Textron."

SEC: "At the time that you placed the phone call to Textron did you actually believe that there could be a possible offer that was in the works for Textron?"

Levine: "I characterized it both to Mr. Waters and Mr. Dolan [Beverly Dolan, Textron's CEO], to whom I spoke that day, that this was only a rumor—and more often than not these things never materialize—and I would not be too alarmed. . . . I would continue to monitor and again characterized it only as a rumor."

SEC: "Would you please recount the entire conversation that you had with Mr. Dolan on that occasion that you and Mr. Waters had with him?"

Levine: "Steve, who has a relationship with Mr. Dolan, as the merger-and-acquisition partner of the firm, handles the Textron account for the firm. [He] led the conversation by saying that his colleague, me, Dennis Levine, has picked up a rumor that Textron may be the subject of an unsolicited offer and we thought it would be wise to bring this to his attention.

"We mentioned we think there might be somebody accumulating the stock, that the stock was trading up that day in a down market and once again we cautioned him that this was only a rumor and we would continue to monitor it and report back any additional information as available."

SEC: "And what response, if any, did Mr. Dolan have?"

Levine: "He told us, as I recall, that it was the first time he heard of it and he thanked us very much for the call.

"He also encouraged us to continue to call him if we had any additional information."

SEC: "Was there any discussion of the possible retention of Lehman Brothers in this conversation by Textron?"

Levine: "I don't recall."

SEC: "Did Mr. Dolan appear to be concerned or worried by the information that you provided?"

Levine: "No."

SEC: "Other than encouraging you to provide further information that you got, did Mr. Dolan request that Lehman Brothers do anything?"

Levine: "No."

SEC: "At the conclusion of this call with Mr. Dolan did you and Mr. Waters have any further conversation on the subject of Textron?"

Levine: "Yes."

SEC: "And what was the further conversation that you had?"

Levine: "I told Mr. Waters that I would continue to monitor the stock and I asked him what the likelihood of our working with him would be, should something happen. I recall his response to me was that Bev—this is Bev Dolan—is a very straight guy and we had worked with him in the past and the chances were very good. . . ."

SEC: "After this conversation with Mr. Waters, what if anything did you do thereafter or what did you continue to do with respect to Textron?"

Levine: "Based on Mr. Waters's input that there was a high probability that we could work with him, I thought it would be useful to commence the preparation of a standard presentation on defensive strategy and advice on unsolicited offers."

SEC: "And was this standard presentation in fact prepared?"

Levine: "Yes."

SEC: "Did you take any steps to acquire further information

as to the possibility of an unsolicited offer for Textron?"

Levine: "No."

SEC: "Are you aware of anyone from Lehman Brothers after
the initial call to Mr. Dolan continuing to have contact
with Textron?"

Levine: "Yes."

SEC: "As far as you were aware, when was the next time
after the first call to Mr. Dolan that anyone from
Lehman Brothers had contact with Textron?"

Levine: "I think about a week later. It was Waters and myself, we called him again. We said there doesn't seem
to be any aberrant trading and, in fact, there may not
be somebody buying the stock. We indicated that there
was a group and this was probably not a corporate
buyer. I believe we may have speculated on who the
participants in the group might be."

SEC: "What was that speculation?"

Levine: "It was the likes of Carl Icahn, Saul Steinberg, Victor Posner, Ivan Boesky and other predator types."

Here we see the connection between the investment bankers
who try to push the companies into play and the corporate raiders
whose very names elicit fear in corporate management. Knowing
that a Saul Steinberg is out to acquire a company or that an Ivan
Boesky is gobbling its stock prompts management to take defensive action. That would include hiring an investment firm. Thus
the pressure on Dolan by the Lehman group. After a series of
additional calls attempting to keep Dolan edgy about a possible
takeover and thus enlist him as a Lehman client, Levine, who
knew exactly what was brewing, turned up the heat.

SEC: "And after this second conversation in which you discussed the activity in the market, did you have any
subsequent conversation with Mr. Dolan?"

Levine: ". . . I called him later that day when the volume
was inordinately high and I said, 'Bev, it's very clear

that something is going on.' He said, 'We'll all find out together.'"

SEC: "Was that all of the conversation?"

Levine: "No, I had one more conversation with Mr. Dolan which I recall was very late in the day, at which point I told him that we picked up from another source that they were about to get an offer from a company called Chicago Pacific."

This "source" was none other than Robert Wilkis.

SEC: "Did you tell Mr. Dolan anything about a price for an offer?"

Levine: "Greater than forty dollars per share."

SEC: "And are you aware as to what this other source was?"

Levine: "It was an arb."

SEC: "Did you have any contact with this arb?"

Levine: "A call came in to Lehman Brothers from an arb and was transferred to me since it was my responsibility to ferret out these types of calls. The secretary asked would I take a call from an arb on Textron and I said that I definitely would.

"So he got on and said, 'Are you guys involved in Textron?' I said, 'Why do you ask? What do you know?' He said, 'You're the banker of record and we hear that they're getting an offer.' I said, 'I see that in the market, but do you know anything additional?' He said he heard it was Chicago Pacific."

SEC: "Who was this arb?"

Levine: "I don't remember who it was."

After additional questioning, the SEC lawyers pressed Levine about his possible stake in Textron shares, only to hear a series of outrageous lies. Sudden memory lapses like his are common in government investigations.

SEC: "Prior to October 24 had you gotten any indication as to any involvement on the part of the firm of Lazard Frères [Wilkis's employer] as to any possible offer for

Textron?"

Levine: "No."

SEC: "Since April 1, 1984, have you personally transacted any Textron stock or options for Textron?"

Levine: "No."

SEC: "Or have you transacted in any securities of Textron?"

Levine: "No."

SEC: "Are you aware if your wife has?"

Levine: "She has not."

SEC: "Are you aware of the identities of anybody who has transacted in Textron stock or options or securities since April 1, 1984?"

Levine: "Not specifically."

SEC: "Do you maintain accounts with any Swiss financial institutions?"

Levine: "No."

SEC: "Have you within the last year maintained any Swiss accounts?"

Levine: "No."

SEC: "Do you have any signature authority or authority to direct trading with respect to any accounts at any Swiss financial institutions?"

Levine: "No."

SEC: "Have you within the last year?"

Levine: "No."

SEC: "Are you aware if your wife has any accounts with any Swiss financial institutions?"

Levine: "She does not."

SEC: "Are you aware if she has had such account within the last year or had authority over such an account within the last year?"

Levine: "She has not."

SEC: "With whom besides your counsel have you talked about the fact that you are appearing here today, if anybody?"

Levine: "Nobody. My wife."

SEC: "No one at Lehman Brothers knows?"

> *Levine:* "Oh, Judith MacDonald, who is our internal coun-
> sel. Of course, I tell Mr. Solomon everything and Mr.
> Waters also knows."
> *SEC:* "What was the conversation you had with Mr. Solomon
> about the fact that you were appearing here today?"
> *Levine:* "I indicated to Mr. Solomon that I had been sub-
> poenaed by the SEC in the matter of Textron and he
> asked me in what regard. I told him it related to the
> trading of the stock. He said, did I ever speak to the
> SEC before, and I told him no. He said, 'Tell them the
> truth; give them the facts and you'll have no problem.'"

Statements by SEC commissioner Joseph A. Grundfest are surprisingly relevant to Levine's first testimony before the SEC. In a
speech to the National Investor Relations Institute on June 20,
1980, Grundfest made these remarks:

"[A] concern that has been bandied about is that the Commission will pursue individuals who trade on the basis of innocently
overheard inside information. Typically, the hypothetical is put
something like this: 'I'm in an airport waiting lounge, or bar, or
elevator of an office building, and overhear these two guys talking
about the big deal they're going to announce on Friday. If I trade
on that information, will I get sued by the SEC?'

"Realistically, if that's what actually happened, the odds are
that you're safe from enforcement action. Unfortunately, these
stories are often designed to cover clear misappropriations or
breaches of fiduciary duty. In fact, the story that 'I heard it in a
bar, elevator or airport' is up there with 'The dog ate my home-
work' as a credible explanation for trading in many of our investigations. . . .

"At its roots, however, any such casual-encounter story is fun-
damentally implausible. How many of you would really invest a
substantial portion of your net worth in highly volatile stocks or
options [on the basis of] something overheard from two total
strangers? How many of you would overhear such chats more
than once, and invest more than once?

"In a word, if you're going to claim the dog ate your home-work, it's probably a good idea to at least own a dog. Many de-fendants we encounter with this story don't."

In this first encounter with the SEC, Levine got away scot-free. Finding no reason to doubt his Textron alibi and having no addi-tional evidence to refute his story, the SEC let the matter drop. Levine was not a suspect.

"We took Dennis's testimony on the Textron case as a player in the transaction, not as an inside trader," says SEC enforce-ment chief Gary Lynch, excusing this agency's embarrassing oversight. "At the time, we hadn't isolated him as a possible trader. So we interviewed him and let him go."

In all likelihood, Levine assumed that was the beginning and the end of the Textron affair—that once again he had outsmarted the system and emerged the stronger for it. He had surmised from the episode that the SEC was a paper tiger—nothing to be con-cerned about.

Sometime later, as the SEC was closing in on Bank Leu and in turn on Levine, he discussed the Textron incident with Bruno Pletscher, who recalled the conversation this way.

SEC: "You indicated that Mr. X advised you that you could go into the SEC and in effect tell a false story and that the SEC would not be able to do anything about it. Did he indicate to you a basis for why he thought that was a likely result?"

Pletscher: "Yes. Mr. X told us that he has experience with the SEC, and he and people that he knows have been called to the SEC for testimonies. Mr. X then said, 'You just tell the SEC what you want to tell them,' and he and other people went there before, just lied to the SEC and walked out without any problem, since the SEC does not have any proof. . . ."

But in his disdain for those he considered lowly bureaucrats, Levine underestimated at least one of the men across the table at the SEC—one who ultimately would bring him to the mat.

"I like to solve puzzles," says Lynch, a ten-year SEC veteran whose shaggy school-boy hair and German shepherd eyes make him look both gentle and tough. "That's why I came to the SEC a year out of law school and why the job still thrills me. In this business, you can't be a person who says, 'Now I've arrived at work, so I'll start thinking about my work. And now I'm leaving the office, so I'll stop thinking about work.' To be good in this business you have to wake up in the middle of the night saying, 'Something's going on here. Something I don't understand. What is it? Why did that guy do what he did?' You have to live your work."

Lynch's investigation into insider trading would continue for another eighteen months before the name Dennis Levine surfaced again. When it did, it brought on the most shocking scandal in Wall Street history. When that scandal broke, making the front pages of *The New York Times* and *The Wall Street Journal*, not even Lynch and his colleagues at the SEC would guess that the mid-echelon investment banker they had questioned about the Textron case and had nabbed for his own multimillion-dollar inside trading would ultimately lead them to the elusive arbitrage community and its most infamous member, Ivan Boesky.

VI

Trading Secrets: Arbitragers and the Wall Street Grapevine

"I think greed is healthy. You can be greedy and still feel good about yourself."
> —*Arbitrager Ivan Boesky in a 1985 commencement speech to the Berkeley School of Business Administration*

The closer you look, the more you see that Wall Street leaks like a sieve. For every swatch of secret information, for every confidential report, there is a temptation to leak it and a determined source trying to pry it out. No one is better at getting that information than the arbitragers.

The undisputed high rollers in the M&A business, arbs bet enormous sums of capital that a deal will or will not go through and thus that the stocks involved will or will not go up or down. The arbs base their livelihood on the ability to obtain critical information.

"They're the cross-pollinators of Wall Street," says a Drexel Burnham investment banker who fields at least a dozen arb calls a day. "In this little corner of the world, where everyone needs information to succeed, the arbs carry that information from one party to the next—always with an IOU attached.

"Take lawyer Krotchet whose client Amalgamated Fenders fears that Jaws Industries is after his company. Amalgamated orders Krotchet to defend the company from this unfriendly suitor. If he's worth his salt, the first thing Krotchet does before rushing out to the pharmacy for an order of poison pills is find out if Jaws is really plotting a move or if Amalgamated has simply come down with a bad case of takeover phobia.

"Where does Krotchet turn? To Jaws? Maybe but, again, if he's had any experience at this game, he knows not to expect the truth there. So where? You've got it, your friendly neighborhood arb. How does the arb know what Jaws is up to? Because a JAWS investment banker, who needed and got similar information from the arb only weeks before and now owes the arb payment in kind, sort of leaked the word of a pending takeover—a leak that, because of the banker's strategy, was in his client's interest. What do we have here? In two deals advance information gets out, and in both cases it gets to the arbs first."

Asked about the propriety of all this, the arbs also talk about "cross-pollination," holding that they play a pivotal role in the securities markets, enabling the principals in M&A transactions to communicate with one another through an impromptu party line. To provide that function, some arbs say (although never for the record) they must be free to talk with insiders, even if that means gaining an advantage in sniffing out market news.

But what precisely do the arbs do? How do they profit from or, in some cases, lose in mergers and acquisitions? On what basis do they make their investments?

Ivan Boesky, who was recognized as a shrewd arb even in those deals in which he didn't have inside information, offers the following unusually candid description of the arb process.* (Other arbs guard their method as closely as Coca-Cola guards its soft-drink formula.)

1. Company A offers to exchange one share of its stock, currently selling at $50 per share, for each share of Company B's stock, now selling at $30, upon consummation of the proposed merger in three months.
2. The arbitrageur researches the merger deal to determine what the probability is that the merger will be consummated. ·
3. Upon determining that the probability of consummation is very high, the arbitrager offers the shareholders of Company B $43 a share, payable immediately.

*This list is from the back cover of Boesky's book, *Merger Mania*, New York: Holt, Rinehart & Winston, 1985.

4. Company B shareholders now have two choices: (a) sell immediately to the arbitrageur at $43, thereby realizing an overnight profit of $13; or (b) wait three months and accept in exchange Company A shares now trading at $50. While the latter choice could yield an additional $7 [per share], it would do so only if the merger is consummated and the value of Company A's shares remains at $50.

5. Company B shareholders decide not to wait, and accept the arbitrageur's immediate offer of $43.

6. The arbitrageur buys Company B stock at $43 and immediately sells Company A stock short at $50, thereby locking in a $7-per-share profit, provided the merger is consummated.

7. Three months later the merger is completed, as the arbitrageur's research had indicated it would be.

8. The arbitrageur now exchanges his Company B shares for Company A shares and uses the newly acquired Company A shares to cover his short sales.

9. The arbitrageur's profit is $7 on a three-month investment of $43, thus realizing an annualized return of 65.1 percent.

No one has ever practiced this procedure more successfully in the real world than the ubiquitous Mr. Boesky. The first man to develop a major independent arbitrage fund (as opposed to an arm of an existing investment house), Boesky took enormous positions in hundreds of stocks, flirted with others and was rumored to be involved with still more. Because of his huge investments, which by themselves could drive stock prices up or down, and because of his extraordinary success in the market, which was based only in part on inside information, word that Boesky was in or out of a stock caused others to follow suit. In a community studded with brilliant and successful people, he was clearly a dominant force.

But how did he get there and how did he build his business into a Wall Street powerhouse? Apparently his start in the arbitrage profession came only after everything else failed. The son of a Russian immigrant who owned a Detroit delicatessen, young Ivan worked part-time in the family business, drove an ice cream truck and muddled his way through high school as only a fair student. Although later in life, when cultivating a proper image became almost as important as stockpiling ever greater wealth, he would boast that he had attended Cranbrook, a private school in a suburb of Detroit, most of his high school years were actually spent in public schools—a part of his history he preferred to rewrite.

Moving on to college with about as much interest in higher education as he had in his father's deli, Boesky struggled through a succession of schools; he spent a term at the University of Michigan before graduating from the Detroit College of Law in 1964. After working for a year as a clerk to a federal judge, Boesky made the rounds at Detroit's top law firms, only to find that the doors were closed to a so-so student from a pedestrian school. In many ways, Boesky's experiences mirror those of his cohort Dennis Levine, who also worked his way up from the middle class.

With the handwriting on the wall, Boesky accepted a job with the Detroit office of Big Eight CPA firm Touche Ross. Although the practice of law would not be Boesky's forte, his higher education produced two important results. It was during his school years that he married Seema Silberstein, a wealthy and pampered woman whose father, real estate tycoon Ben Silberstein (who thought Boesky to be a poor choice for a husband) owned the Beverly Hills Hotel. It was also during his school years that he had a roommate whose subsequent fascination with arbitrage rubbed off on Boesky, later convincing him to head for Wall Street.

Moving with Seema to New York, Boesky started his own arbitrage partnership in 1975, funding the venture with $350,000 from his wife's mother and stepfather and an equal amount of his own and Seema's money. With a budding reputation for shrewdly picking takeover stocks, he quickly drew wealthy investors into the fold. They were rewarded for their faith. In about four years, the partnership's capital grew from its initial seed money to almost $100 million. Net income in 1979 alone approached $60 million.

But this turned out to be the zenith. Proving that even the great Boesky was vulnerable to the roller-coaster swings of arbitrage, Ivan the Terrible, as he came to be known, stubbed his toe on a series of major deals; the partnership's capital plummeted by about $40 million in 1980. With net earnings also collapsing to about $10 million, Boesky severed his relationship with the arb partnership, only to reemerge in 1981 as the head of an arbitrage corporation. This was the first of several reincarnations of his arbitrage business during the 1980s. While there continued to be such periodic losses as a $24 million drop in Cities Service stock when Gulf Oil withdrew a bid for the company and a $70 million hemorrhage when T. Boone Pickens withdrew a bid for Phillips Petroleum, the gains outweighed the setbacks. Profits like the $65 million gain when Chevron went after Gulf enriched his investors and reinforced Boesky's reputation as a prodigious moneymaker.

A vice-president with Drexel Burnham Lambert, the investment banking firm that raised the money for Boesky's most recent limited partnership and has been involved with him in a number of questionable transactions, put it this way:

"More than anyone else down here, Ivan has the ability to coin money. His extensive network of sources, his incredible feel for the market, and his uncanny sense of timing—put it all together and you have a man [who] comes pretty close to performing miracles. How else do you describe turning a million into a hundred million? Ivan's done it more than once.

"Look at it this way: some of the shrewdest people in this country—and I'm talking about people who, in spite of their wealth, are tough with a buck—put their money with Ivan. Not because they like him or because he plays good squash. It's because over the years, even accounting for the dips in his performance, he's made them richer than they already were."

As smart and shrewd as his partners may have been, Boesky

always used them to his own advantage, cutting deals with the investors (and later with the SEC) that have assured him a lopsided return. In an August 1984 analysis of the arbitrage corporation Boesky formed in 1981, *Fortune* magazine found that "the corporation has two classes of equity: preferred and common. Preferred holders receive fixed dividends, which last year totaled less than 3 percent of net profits. After these, the preferred holders received 45 percent of net profit, which goes to their retained earnings account. Common stockholders get 55 percent, also held in retained earnings. As of last February, outside investors owned 82 percent of the preferred stock but only 2 percent of the common. So as the arithmetic works out, outside investors got 38 percent of the year's profits versus 62 percent for Boesky.

"When fate turns against the company, however, Boesky gets off relatively easy, while outside investors get soaked. Boesky Corp's preferred holders bear 95 percent of all losses; common holders bear only 5 percent."*

So were the investors fools to participate with Boesky?

"Only small minds would see it that way," says the Drexel Burnham VP. "As long as you're making a lot of money with him, what's the difference how much Ivan's squirreling away for himself? The truth is he deserves the king's portion. As the mastermind of the firm's investments, as the guy who knows what to buy and when to sell it better than anyone else—or they'd be doing it themselves—he's entitled to a disproportionate share of the take. Arbitrage isn't a democracy. It's a meritocracy."

In 1986, the head of the meritocracy restructured his main trading vehicle again, liquidating Ivan F. Boesky Corp. In the process, he withdrew $193 million for himself and created a limited partnership, Ivan F. Boesky & Co., L.P. For this venture, Drexel Burham raised $660 million, the largest pool of capital ever assembled for arbitrage. The investors, including forty-three limited partners and forty debenture holders, included a mix of

* Gwen Kinkead, "Ivan Boesky, Money Machine," *Fortune*, August 6, 1984, p. 104.

wealthy individuals, financial institutions and pension funds. Britain's Water Authorities Superannuation Fund went for $10 million, Lincoln National Life risked $10 million and Gould's pension fund invested $5.7 million.

Here again, the take was tilted to Boesky. Although he had only a small stake of $13 million in the company, the founder was entitled to 40 percent of the profits plus substantial fees paid to him as the fund's general partner and investment adviser. Too big a bite? Again, many said no.

"Investors know that great arbs perform magic," the Drexel Burnham executive says. "And that's something you just can't put a price tag on."

But what's behind the arb's magic? How does a major arbitrager decide where to invest his money at those times when he doesn't have the benefit of a paid informant? How does he decide if a prospective takeover merits a capital investment or if the potential rewards outweigh the risks?

Here another prominent arb, Prudential-Bache's Guy Wyser-Pratte, flings open the shutters, casting daylight on what might be called the "arb analysis."

There is a definite and fairly common sequence to the arbitrager's financial analysis which allows him to arrive at his investment decision. He

    (a) gathers information about the particular deal;

    (b) calculates the value of the securities offered;

    (c) determines the length of time he can expect his capital to be tied up in the deal;

    (d) calculates his expected per annum return on invested capital;

    (e) determines and weighs all the possible risks and problem areas which might preclude consummation of the transaction;

    (f) assesses the various tax implications and establishes his tax strategy;

    (g) determined the amount of stock available for borrow-
        ing in order to be able to sell short;

    (h) determines the amount of capital to be committed to
        the deal [on the basis of] careful balancing of (a)
        through (g) above.*

The first step, gathering "information about the particular deal," is critical to the arbitrage function. As the arbs say, "He who learns first profits first; he who learns second, may not profit at all." The uncanny ability to gain information before others and to make savvy use of this scoop has always been a trademark of the arbitragers.

"The notable London merchant bank of Rothschild, as the story goes, staged an unprecedented *coup de bourse* by use of carrier pigeons to receive advance notice of Wellington's victory at Waterloo," Wyser-Pratte's *Risk Arbitrage II* relates. "Upon learning the news, Rothschild began, with much ado, selling various securities, particularly British government bonds, on the London Stock Exchange. This was naturally interpreted as a Wellington defeat, thereby precipitating a panicky selling wave. The astute and informed Rothschild then began purchasing, through stages, all the government bonds that were for sale. When an earthbound messenger finally brought the news of an allied victory, Rothschild had a handsome profit."

Today, with carrier pigeons hardly providing an advantage and with all the parties to a deal having equal access to the Dow Jones wire, arbs must rely on networks of personal contacts in and out of the arb community and on their ability to pry the truth from the parties to the deal.

Wyser-Pratte puts it this way in his book: "It is often best to hear from the companies themselves the purported reasons for their proposed merger. It is at this point that the curtain rises on

*Guy Wyser-Pratte, *Risk Arbitrage II*, copyright 1982 New York University and Guy Wyser-Pratte, p. 7.

one of the great comic operas of Wall Street: obtaining information from the involved companies about their proposed merger. It is indeed comic because the companies will always present a rosy prognosis for the successful consummation of their proposed marriage, while the arbitrage community, always suspicious, will, in their conversations with the companies, try to draw out the hard and cold facts about the real state of affairs: the actual stage of the negotiations as well as the matter of business logic. . . .

"Approaching companies to gather information is ticklish for the arbitrager. He must tailor his approach on whether he is interrogating the Bride or the Groom. The Bride is normally totally cooperative, realizing that the arbitrager can, by purchasing her stock, accumulate votes which will naturally be cast in favor of the merger. So, to the Bride, the arbitrager can candidly state his business. The Groom is an entirely different matter. He will not be pleased that his stock may become the subject of constant short selling by arbitragers; he is thus often elusive in his response. To counteract this, the arbitrager must often become the 'wolf in sheep's clothing' by assuming the role of the investment banker who seems to be desirous of assisting the Groom with his acquisition program—both the present proposed merger and future plans.

"In this manner the arbitrager ingratiates himself with the host in order to ask those delicate questions about the pending merger negotiations. The arbitrager may also don the garb of the institutional salesman who is attempting to place with institutional investors the new securities which may be offered to the Bride. If he is to sell those securities effectively, he must know the details of the merger, particularly the date when these securities will be issued, which will coincide roughly with the closing of the merger transaction. Not surprisingly, most Grooms with active acquisition programs are well aware of the guises of the arbitrager. Some cooperate; others don't."

Seated in his elegantly furnished twenty-sixth-floor office complete with a brass telescope pointed at a sweeping view of New York harbor, Wyser-Pratte splits his vision between a visitor and

115

a huge Quotron terminal. A second-generation arb—his father sold the family business, Wyser-Pratte & Co., to Prudential Insurance in 1967—Guy is proud of his profession ("the second oldest in the world") and insists that it can and should be performed without the benefit of inside information.

Wyser-Pratte is clearly perturbed that the insider trading scandals have cast aspersions on the arbs, portraying them as devious operators wired to a hotline of inside information. In comments made shortly before the Ivan Boesky scandal broke, he insisted that the other M&A players—some of whom he holds in contempt—are far more culpable than his brethren.

"I think everybody would like to give the impression that the problem of insider trading is with the arbitragers, because it takes the focus off of everybody else. But it seems to me that the people who consistently get indicted or nailed are the corporate directors, their fellow travelers, investment bankers and lawyers.

"What arbitragers do and shouldn't do is a matter of common sense. You shouldn't try to get inside information, and if you get it you shouldn't utilize it."

But what of the Wall Street consensus that arbs spend their days connected to a bank of telephones by which they cajole, gossip and whisper with the very players who, as Wyser-Pratte so bluntly puts it, get "nailed" for insider trading? If the arbs aren't playing the insider game too, what are they talking about to the corporate directors, the investment bankers, the lawyers and the proxy solicitors?

"The investment bankers call us—rather than the other way around—because they need help putting together the deals they're supposed to be putting together themselves," Wyser-Pratte fires back, revealing his disdain for the men in suspenders and Hermes ties. "Most investment bankers are ignorant of the marketplace, and arbitragers have to price deals every day, ten times a day. We have to make investment decisions and get an automatic readout within five minutes of what we are doing. So we're in a position that the investment bankers wouldn't dream of being in their entire lives. It's the arbitragers who actually take the positions and take the risks. The investment bankers need our feel of the market and our experience in takeovers.

"But frankly, I don't think there should be any contact between arbitragers and investment bankers at all. What would happen if we didn't talk? You'd see the arbitragers functioning just like they've always functioned and the investment bankers out on a limb."

No communication with investment bankers, the principal players in mergers and acquisitions? In a utopian world, perhaps, but not on modern Wall Street. That the arb community is infested with as many inside traders as the corporate boards and the investment banks is made clear by dual scandals that rocked the profession within months of each other.

The first, coming on the heels of Dennis Levine's arrest, involved superyuppies Michael David and Andrew Solomon, twenty-seven-year-old East Side New Yorkers with a collection of degrees from Wharton, Stanford and the University of Chicago, and memberships at a hip Manhattan Nautilus nest, the Vertical Club. Introduced by Drexel Burnham arbitrage analyst Robert Salsbury at one of the after-work functions that are Wall Street's version of the happy hour, the two became fast friends, lunching and brunching and working out together. They later spent a good deal of time burning up the telephone lines between their respective offices.

Though both had been trained as lawyers, neither was smitten with the practice of law. After a revolving-door apprenticeship at the law firm of Weil, Gotshal & Manges, Solomon, who had always carried a torch for Wall Street, segued over to the small but prominent arbitrage firm of Marcus Schloss & Company, where he would analyze potential investments.

David, equally restless, moved from an abortive start as a real estate associate at the law firm of Roseman Colin Freund Lewis & Cohen, where he made less than a stellar impression, to another premier law firm, Paul, Weiss, Rifkind, Wharton & Garrison, where his lack of performance and acute uninterest were apparent to the partners and to his peers. Like Solomon's, David's true love was finance, a field he courted by dialing a network of young arbs, among them Solomon, and spouting his opinions on pending corporate transactions, some of which involved Paul, Weiss clients. His objective was to impress the arbs with his prescience, to be included in their information pipeline, and ultimately to gain a ticket out of Paul, Weiss and into an arb house.

In time, David and Solomon recognized that their needs and objectives were in perfect sync. David, seeking the arb connection, was eager to impress Solomon with his knowledge. Solomon, ordered by his superiors at Marcus Schloss to vacuum the Street for news, tidbits, whispers and rumors on pending deals, was eager to hear David's monologue. If the Paul, Weiss associate had inside information to reveal, so much the better. Arb firms pay handsomely for results, nothing for ethics.

Soon enough, according to government charges, inside information would be forthcoming. In early December 1985 David learned that a Paul, Weiss client, GAF, was planning a tender offer for the beleaguered Union Carbide Corporation. He called Solomon, tipping him off to the pending deal. Within forty-eight hours, Solomon and a partner at Marcus Schloss purchased more than 10,000 Union Carbide shares.

Their initial tip was followed by a series of leaks concerning a number of Paul, Weiss's clients including Dominion Textile, which was planning to take over Avondale Mills, and Damson Oil, which was being sought by Seaborg. David didn't stop with Solomon but extended his illegal telegraph service to Drexel Burnham's Salsbury; to twenty-four-year-old stockbroker Morton Shapiro who, along with Salsbury, lived in the same apartment building as David; and to one of Shapiro's customers, twenty-three-year-old Daniel Silverman.

In one case, David learned of a possible takeover of American Brands by the Paul, Weiss's British-based client B.A.T. Industries. He informed Shapiro on March 9, 1985, and the broker then purchased option contracts in American Brands for himself,

David and Silverman, all through the account he managed for Silverman. Within days, the three unloaded their options for a profit of about $140,000. It is unclear what happened to this money. Most of it may have been used to offset losses in previous trades.

According to the indictment, while the three were dabbling in options, Solomon was earning his stripes at Marcus Schloss, prompting the firm to take a 7,500-share position in the stock. Soon afterward, Schloss was able to sell about half of its stake, for a twenty-four-hour profit of about $9,800. Marcus Schloss executives, for their part, deny that any of their purchases were made because of information supplied by David.

As effortless as the insider trading game may have looked at this point, it was about to unravel. Something happened that none of the participants could have anticipated: a Wall Street executive actually took inside trading seriously enough to report his discoveries to authorities. In the process he would lose his job and with it his reputation on the Street. The only nonparticipant to blow the whistle voluntarily on the current spate of M&A leaks, he would pay a heavier penalty than some of the perpetrators of inside trading.

The whistleblower, Arthur Ainsberg, served as chief compliance and financial officer at Marcus Schloss. An alumnus of the Wall Street–savvy accounting firm of Oppenheim, Appel, Dixon, he had the accountant's nose for impropriety and the moral conviction to do something about it. Suspicious of Solomon because he brought tips to the trading room immediately after receiving telephone calls, Ainsberg asked the young analyst how he had learned about the American Brands rumor. To Ainsberg's amazement, Solomon apparently bragged that someone at Paul, Weiss was leaking news to him.

"To me, that proves that Solomon thought he was operating in an environment—the business of arbitrage—where inside trading is not only condoned, but viewed as a sign that the guy is connected, that he's valuable to his firm," says a partner with Arthur Young, another active Wall Street CPA firm. "There's no other explanation for boasting about illegal activities to the god-damn compliance officer. You only do that if you think it's going to put more zeroes in your bonus."

But Solomon got more (or less) than he bargained for. Determined to get hard evidence, Ainsberg set a trap, inviting Solomon to his apartment for dinner on March 14, 1986. Shortly before his unsuspecting guest arrived for what he thought would be a pleasant repast, Ainsberg inserted a blank tape into a pocket Dictaphone and then slipped the recorder into his pocket. Moments later, by appearing impressed with his guest's ability to gain information, Ainsberg would trick Solomon into revealing his ties to Michael David.

From then on, events moved quickly. Ainsberg was led by Solomon to believe that certain Marcus Schloss executives had known all along of the Paul, Weiss connection (there is no evidence, however, that this is true), and he feared taking the tape to his employers. Instead, he made contact with a Paul, Weiss senior partner, who listened to the tape and concluded that the firm had suffered a serious breach of client confidence. With Ainsberg asking for time to find legal counsel of his own, the evidence was temporarily withheld from the SEC. In the meantime, Paul, Weiss shipped David off to Paris to work on what he was led to believe was an important client matter, in order to remove him from the scene without arousing his suspicions.

On March 25 Ainsberg and his counsel, Alvin Hellerstein of Stroock & Stroock & Lavan handed the tape over to the SEC's New York boss Ike Sorkin. The next day, David, who had returned from Paris, was fired from Paul, Weiss. Within hours, Solomon was nabbed by the Feds and hustled down to the U.S. Attorney's Office, where securities-fraud chief Charles Carberry laid down the law: the young arb would cooperate or get the book thrown at him. Knowing he was "in the shit" (as Bank Leu's Bernhard Meier put it), Solomon agreed to be wired and to meet immediately with David and Salsbury for the purpose of getting hard evidence against them. With the tape rolling, he got both men to talk about the scheme. With that, federal agents moved in on the former Paul, Weiss associate and, after he refused to co-operate, threw him in jail for the night.

The investigation continued over the following months, culminating in indictments on May 28 against David, Solomon, Salsbury, Shapiro and Silverman. On June 5 all the defendants except David pleaded guilty. The former Paul, Weiss associate and alleged mastermind of the trading ring pleaded guilty in December. In court Salsbury and Solomon stated that senior executives at their firms, Drexel Burnham and Marcus Schloss, respectively, were aware that they had passed along inside information and had traded on that basis—charges both firms denied.

Meanwhile, Ainsberg, whose identity as the whistleblower was revealed earlier in an SEC complaint, found himself without a job. "Arthur paid a price for doing what was right," says one of Ainsberg's attorneys, Melvin Brosterman, a partner with Stroock & Stroock & Lavan. "Since resigning from Marcus Schloss, where he felt he could no longer work in good conscience, he has found it difficult to find a position equal to the one he had at the firm."

Although cracking what was dubbed the Yuppie Five case brought joy to the U.S. Attorney's Office and to the SEC, which was clearly on a roll after the Dennis Levine breakthrough, the word on Wall Street was that the Feds had amused themselves with bit players while the real kingfish of the arb community were doing business as usual—collecting inside information from an extended family of corporate directors, investment bankers, lawyers and assorted informants, all stoking the rumor mill for their own self-interest.

In this context, everyone was thinking Ivan Boesky. As the Street's most flamboyant and successful arb, the man hot-wired into more prominent figures than anyone else, the one with the longest string of investment bull's-eyes, he was at the top of two lists—those most likely to be inside traders and those least likely to be indicted for it.

A Drexel Burnham merger executive echoed the sentiment of

many on the Street: "Boesky's up to his ass in inside information. Look, you work here long enough and you know, instinctively or [through] the grapevine, what's going on. And in this case both tell you that Ivan's got inside sources. . . . First, everyone speaks to Ivan. They want his thoughts on this, his opinion on that. He gives it and in return he asks the same from others. Because he's so important, and so connected, no one wants to say no to Ivan.

"Second, Ivan and Drexel are tangled up in one another like two branches of the same big family. We raised the money for his limited-partnership arbitrage firm, Ivan F. Boesky & Co., L.P. Many of the investors in it are also our junk-bond clients and we own part of his West Coast hotel operation, the Northview Corp. That means he's got access here and, as you know, this place is chock-full of gold-plated secrets. How hard would it be for him to find out about the deals we're working on? Not hard at all.

"Third, Ivan's been too successful. Too many of his buys go through the roof as soon as the order clears. No one's that smart. He's got to be getting help."

If it was common knowledge on the Street that Ivan Boesky was one of the biggest, most successful inside traders, why didn't the SEC know it? According to the same Drexel Burnham executive, they did.

"They've known it for years. I hear they've investigated dozens of his trades but it's never come to anything and it never will. Because Ivan Boesky's too powerful, too cozy with too many big hitters here and in Washington. And God, the guy gives money—ten million here, ten million there. No one wants to be cut off from that. Not congressmen or senators or even presidents. Powers of that magnitude don't go to jail."

Asked about Paul Thayer, who though a presidential appointee still went to jail, the executive responds: "Thayer was a corporate executive with a nice job and a nice salary. Ivan Boesky is a pillar of capitalism with billions of dollars under his control. Next to Boesky, Thayer is just another working stiff. To make it look good, the government may investigate Boesky, but they don't really want to find anything on him."

After investigating Ivan the Terrible for three years, from 1983 to 1986, and probing into forty-seven of his arbitrage transactions, the SEC and the New York Stock Exchange came up empty-handed. Wall Street's leading arbitrager was free to operate as he saw fit, thriving in a laissez-faire environment that seemed unable to decipher his methods or to restrain them in any way. But for much of the time he was, as the Drexel executive suspected, trading on inside information. One source was Dennis Levine.

Since his first knowledge of Boesky from press clippings and an occasional glimpse of the infamous arb, surrounded by bodyguards, dashing from one Wall Street building to another, Levine lionized the man. Friends and associates recall Levine's insatiable appetite for stories, anecdotes and rumors about the Wall Street wonder who'd turned a degree from a Motown law school into a luminous career.

"People on the Street love to exaggerate," the Drexel partner continues. "They'll pump up a stock or inflate a fee or embellish a deal so that it takes on epic proportions. That's part of the game.

"But with Boesky, exaggeration wasn't necessary. His life was directed by Cecil B. De Mille. The guy was a walking, talking movie epic. Frank Capra would have loved it too. Poor boy from Detroit, son of a delicatessen owner, muddles through college, comes to Wall Street in 1966 and, after lowly positions with a string of brokerage firms, proceeds to build an empire in arbitrage. Unlike so many of the bow-tied gremlins around here, he does it with style. His main office resembles the flight deck of a space station. The guy's phone console has 286 buttons. Steven Spielberg couldn't ask for more.

"On top of that, the guy appears to be superhuman. At his office by daybreak—sometimes before that. Working through the evening without lunch or cocktails or snacks. All he needs is coffee—sixteen to twenty cups a day. Food and sleep and rest and music—that's for mortals. Not for Ivan Boesky.

"There were always new Boesky stories. How he bought this or sold that or did any number of strange or extraordinary things. But after a while, everyone got tired of hearing it. Everyone but Dennis. He could never get enough Boesky trivia. All the traits that made Ivan strange and weird and eccentric made him enormously appealing to Dennis."

Levine was already building bridges to the arb community, both to create an outside power base and to siphon off leaks and rumors for his inside trading ring, but he knew that his efforts would be incomplete without a Boesky connection.

"But when it came to Boesky, Dennis was driven by more than just money," says the Drexel executive. "He wanted to know Boesky; to be his business partner; to be part of his world. To Dennis, that goal ranked right up there with being rich."

From all indications, the connection was made in February 1985, just after Levine abandoned his Lehman vice-presidency for a Drexel Burnham partnership. Relating to Boesky in the language he understood best and in a way that would instantly ingratiate him with the arbitragers, Dennis began to dole out information on a series of merger negotiations involving Coastal Corporation's offer for American National Resources, Sperry's talks with ITT, and a leveraged buyout of McGraw-Edison— deals on which Levine cleared more than $2 million in profits.

Impressed by the young banker's brand of ESP, Boesky opened the door to his own world a bit wider, giving Levine access to him. Levine seized the opportunity, calling into Boesky's switchboard as many as a dozen times a day. He had a lot to tell. He had legitimate access to Drexel's precious secrets, since as a managing director he was among the first to learn of client machinations. Levine's far-flung illegal trading ring also telegraphed leaks from Lehman Brothers, Goldman Sachs, Lazard Frères and Wachtell, Lipton.

Boesky and Levine both knew Levine had a lot to sell, so beginning in April 1985, they changed the terms of the Levine–Boesky hotline from a gratis service to a profit-making venture. Levine would give Boesky stock tips in return for 5 percent of the profits. Where Levine's scoop influenced Boesky only to hold or to increase existing positions, the commissions would be limited to 1 percent of the gain. Building in a safety net, Boesky provided that his payments would be offset by any losses suffered as a result of Levine's inside tips.

It was a marriage made in heaven—or, in the terminology Wall Street prefers, a "perfect synergy." Each party brought a rich dowry to the union: Levine airtight information and Boesky enormous capital to put this information to maximum advantage.

For Levine and Boesky the serious trading began in the spring of 1985. In April Nabisco Brands hired Lehman Brothers for advice and consultation on a possible merger with R. J. Reynolds, the tobacco giant turned food conglomerate. As a member of Lehman's mergers-and-acquisitions department, Ira Sokolow, a full-fledged member of Levine's information pipeline, tipped off Levine to the pending deal. Levine, who always took care of his own account first, ordered Bank Leu to buy him 150,000 shares of Nabisco and then informed Boesky of the wisdom of doing the same. Confident of his source, the arb went his informant a step better, ordering 377,000 Nabisco shares for his various investment entities.

When Nabisco announced on May 30 that it was talking with Reynolds, Nabisco stock soared. Ultimately, Levine made a $2,694,421 profit and Boesky raked in about $4 million.

In a simultaneous deal, Levine shuffled his personnel like a football coach blessed with a strong bench, this time tapping the services of Robert Wilkis. The opportunity came when Lazard Frères, which was serving as investment banking adviser to Houston Natural Gas, learned in April that the client was the subject of a possible acquisition by InterNorth, a huge pipeline company.

Informed of this, Levine bought 74,800 shares of Houston Natural Gas on April 30 and then walkie-talkied Boesky with the news. The arb, a higher roller than his admiring accomplice, bought 301,800 shares. On May 2, it was announced that InterNorth would acquire Houston Natural Gas. Levine sold for a profit of

$907,655 and Boesky's interests cleared $4.1 million.

Showing just how versatile his team was, Levine allegedly hinged another Boesky tip-off on Goldman Sachs investment banker David Brown. FMC Corporation, a manufacturer of defense and farming equipment, met with Goldman Sachs to explore various ways of restructuring the company. By December client and banker had decided on a recapitalization plan whereby FMC would repurchase shares of its own stock. In Wall Street's version of the buddy system, Brown informed Sokolow in early 1986, and Sokolow notified Levine, who telegraphed Boesky. Acting on this leak, the arb purchased 95,300 FMC shares for his investment entities. On February 22 FMC announced that its board had approved a recapitalization plan and described the terms. Soon after, the stock shot skyward, giving Boesky a profit of $975,000.

The Levine-to-Boesky leaks covered a string of companies, including American Natural Resources, Union Carbide and General Foods. (See the table below.) Ivan the Terrible thus gained a stock-market bonanza of more than $50 million, with one estimate as high as $200 million.

BOESKY–LEVINE TRADES

Target stock	Acquiring company	Announce- ments	Bought (shares)	Sold (shares)	Average profit per share
Houston Natural Gas	InterNorth	5/2/85 merger offer	Levine 4/30/85 (74,800)	5/2/85 (74,800)	$12.13
			Boesky 5/1/85 (301,800)	5/14-15/85 (301,800)	$13.58
Nabisco	R. J. Reynolds	5/30/85 merger talks begin	Levine 5/6/85 (150,000)	5/30/85 (150,000)	$17.96
			Boesky 5/22-29/85 (377,000)	5/30/85 (377,000)	$10.61

FMC	—	2/21/86 reorganization plan announced	Levine didn't trade	—	—
			Boesky[1] 2/18-21/86 (95,300)	2/21/86 (95,300)	$10.23
American Natural Resources	Coastal Corporation	3/4/85 tender offer	Levine 2/14-3/1/85 (145,500)	3/1/85 (145,500)	$9.42
			Boesky[1]	N.A.	N.A.
General Foods	Philip Morris	9/27/85 tender offer	Levine didn't trade	—	—
			Boesky[1] 6/30/85 (166,000)[2]	9/30/85 (166,000)[2]	$29.25[2]
Union Carbide	GAF	12/9/85 tender offer for 48 million shares 1/8/86 offer withdrawn	Levine 12/3/85 (100,000)	12/9/85 (100,000)	$1.27
			Boesky[1]	N.A.	N.A.

[1]SEC complaint says Mr. Boesky traded on inside information provided by Mr. Levine.
[2]SEC 13F filings for Ivan F. Boesky Corp. compiled by CDA Investment Technologies Inc.; profits per share calculated using 9/30/85 closing price.
N.A. = not available
Source: Securities and Exchange Commission documents.

According to the 1- to 5-percent-commission formula, Boesky owed his source $2.4 million, a sum he never paid. Why? To some it is just another expression of the greed that drove an enormously wealthy man to risk his reputation and his freedom for the chance to add a few million dollars to his account. But others see a craftier strategy.

"Before an arb gets involved in a deal—any deal—he plays the 'worst-case game,'" says an investment banker familiar with Boesky and Levine. "This means he asks himself, 'In the worst of all cases, what can go wrong and if it does go wrong, how will it affect me?' Knowing his downside risk is a critical component of the arb's analysis.

"When Boesky went through this exercise for the Levine operation, he figured the worst that could happen was that Levine would get caught and in the process take him down with him.

"Levine's undoing was a risk Boesky could live with—he didn't care a whit about Dennis—but his own hide, well, that was a different matter. So he concocted a little scheme of his own. That is, he wouldn't pay Dennis. Oh, he'd promised to come up with the money and would claim it was only a matter of time—that he had to refigure the commission and the like—but his intention was to leave at least some substantial part of the balance open. Recognizing Levine's incredible greed, Boesky figured that even if the investment banker got caught, he wouldn't turn on his best customer. Not while there was still an unpaid balance out there."

A little-known fact is that Boesky made a secret offer to Levine to become the president of his newly formed limited-partnership arbitrage firm, the one Drexel Burnham helped to finance in early 1986. This job offer may have been part of Boesky's manipulative scheme to keep Levine loyal. Although Levine had decided to accept Boesky's job offer shortly before he was arrested, it is not certain that a job was really waiting for him.

"Once he recognized how good Dennis's information was, Boesky wanted it all to himself," says their mutual acquaintance. "He wanted to be alerted to every transaction and to be alerted first. By creating a bond with Dennis—or the illusion of a bond—he thought he could accomplish that. Were Dennis to think that their fates were tied, that he would soon be part of the Boesky empire, he'd have further self-interest in taking care of Ivan.

"But the fact is that only a fool would think that Boesky really wanted to hire Dennis, because in doing so, he'd be taking him out of investment banking, where he could produce the greatest value. That's like a pimp asking his prettiest girl to stay home and clean the house."

VII

A License to Steal

"For the takeover lawyer inclined to abuse his position, his license to practice law becomes a license to steal."

—An anonymous proxy solicitor

Trust, on Wall Street, means everything and nothing. To those who grew up in an era of gentlemanly practice, when a handshake sealed a deal, trust is as valuable as a seat on the stock exchange. But to others, trust is an invitation to abuse.

It was that way with Ivan Boesky. In a way, he was shielded by the system he tried to rape. For all the noise about compliance departments and computerized surveillance systems, the markets still rely on the honesty of the member firms and on their willingness and ability to police their employees. Perhaps honesty is an outdated notion in a time when financial executives replace desktop family portraits with plaques proclaiming: "He who dies with the most money wins."

Referring to the Big Board's efforts to run a clean house, New York Stock Exchange chairman John Phelan, Jr., holds that "the first line of defense is our member firms. We depend upon them, with their compliance, legal and audit staffs, to pick up the first signs of suspicious trading themselves."

But Phelan admits that this is far from perfect: "In the case of Ivan Boesky, an important link in the system failed."

That's because Boesky, as the chief executive of a member firm, was expected to police himself. With little or no concern for integrity—and with the view that trust is simply an opportunity for abuse—he could break the law with relative impunity.

The truth is that the apparatus designed to weed out and control inside trading is built on a house of cards. Much is vested in the assumption of honesty, and all the other checks and balances are built on it. When that honesty does not exist, the checks and balances come crashing down.

Such is the case with the M&A bar. As defenders of the status quo see it, the presence of first-rate legal minds lends a purifying element to the merger-and-acquisition process, alerting all the participants to their duties and obligations under the securities laws. While this may work in theory, in the real world it is not always the case. Time and again, lawyers and others employed by prestigious law firms have abused their position as insiders, turning confidential information into personal gain.

Dave Hall is an example. The son-in-law and law partner of one of the early M&A pioneers, attorney George Demas, Hall took over their firm when Demas left to pursue real estate interests. Entrusted to carry on what was by all accounts a clean-as-a-whistle practice, Hall soon abused the faith placed in him by his partner, his clients and his profession. A prince of the court proved that in the tempting arena of mergers and acquisitions, he could succumb to greed as easily as any other insider.

Hall's trading activities began when Laclede Steel Company, a St. Louis–based manufacturer of carbon and low-alloy steel, learned in early 1974 that it was the object of a possible takeover by another company that had quietly accumulated 4 percent of its common stock, which was traded over the counter. Eyeing this development nervously, Laclede management grew even more disturbed in May, when it learned that the potential suitor had increased its position to 7.6 percent of the company's stock. Alarmed by this, senior management contacted Hall to review its options in defending against an anticipated tender offer.

In a meeting with Laclede executives on May 10, Hall learned not only of the possible takeover but also of his client's internal projections that indicated net earnings for fiscal 1974 would sky-rocket by at least 400 percent over those of the prior year. With the company performing so well and with a potential acquirer in the wings (neither of which was yet known to the public), Hall made his first purchase of Laclede common, acquiring 300 shares at \$65¾ each. Two days later, at its annual shareholders' meeting on May 16, Laclede management announced the rosy report Hall knew was coming: projected net earnings for 1974 were \$12 to \$14 million, an increase of more than 400 percent over 1973. That same day, Laclede stock jumped to \$83 a share.

Over the next month, Hall, working closely with Laclede management, focused on the possible takeover, exploring ways to thwart the prospective suitor. In his role as an adviser and confidant, Hall discussed with Laclede several antitakeover amendments to its articles of incorporation and by-laws. This culminated in Hall's being invited to attend a special meeting on June 28 to discuss the board's responsibility and actions it might take, in case a tender offer was made.

Before heading out to St. Louis, Hall abused the trust placed in him by purchasing another 250 Laclede shares, which by now had climbed to \$94.50, followed by an additional purchase of 24 shares at \$95 each. By this time Hall had become aware not only of the possible tender offer but also of new calculations that indicated Laclede would surpass its previously announced profit projections, earning \$12 million by the end of the third quarter of 1974. In view of this, management favored a stock split and an increase in regular quarterly dividends—both of which would be recommended to the board.

At the June 28 board meeting, the directors reviewed proposed resolutions and communications to be used in the event of a tender offer. Consideration of the proposals to split stock and increase dividends were put off until the next regularly scheduled meeting in July. Although the suspected takeover did not materialize that summer, the stock (and Hall's 574-share investment in it) continued to rise with news of revised earnings projections—now at \$15 to \$17 million for all of 1974—and on the board's subsequent approval of a 300-percent stock dividend and a 300-percent increase in its regular quarterly cash dividend. The day after the dividend announcement on July 25, Laclede's common stock closed at \$106 per share.

Hall, who had bought his first and biggest stake at $65.75 a share, sold some of his Laclede holdings in October 1974 and in January 1975. Then, after meeting with company management in May 1975—at which time he learned that the steelmaker was projecting a decrease in annual earnings for the year—Hall sold the balance of his stock.

Like junket gamblers after their first big day at a Vegas casino, inside traders are compelled to return to the gaming tables. The take is simply too great to resist. The fever got to Hall. Soon after the Laclede episode, he spotted an odds-on wager with another client, Mosinee Paper, a Wisconsin-based manufacturer of lumber products. Representing Mosinee as its "special shareholder relations counsel" since 1972, Hall had regularly advised management on a number of stock-related issues. In one such instance—in early 1974—Hall advised that the company respond to favorable financial results by declaring a stock dividend and an increase in its cash dividend. In April, the board gave its approval, authorizing 20 percent on the stock dividend and 10 percent on the cash distribution.

Hall faced a similar situation in the first quarter of 1976, when Mosinee, turning in an exceptional performance for the first three months, again considered declaring a stock dividend and an increase in its regular quarterly cash dividend. Invited to attend the corporation's annual meeting on April 21, 1976, Hall flew to Wausau, where he met with company officials at 8:30 in the morning. The agenda included various stockholder matters, the most important being the possibility of stock and cash dividends. Shortly after this private tête-à-tête, Mosinee's board met to approve a 10-percent stock dividend and a 10-percent increase in the regular quarterly cash dividend.

At noon Hall met informally with the board members; half an hour later he purchased 500 shares of Mosinee common stock at $13.75 per share. Later that day the corporation made its first public announcement about its improved earnings picture and the related stock and dividend awards. Buoyed by the news, the stock rose to $15.75 the next day.

Things were heating up. With Mosinee's earnings continuing to climb through the year, there was concern that its stock was undervalued, thus making the company vulnerable to a hostile takeover. On or about November 29 Hall received a copy of a highly confidential report prepared by Mosinee's comptroller and intended for submission to the executive committee of the board of directors. In this communication the comptroller recommended that dividend payments to the company's shareholders be increased.

On December 9 Hall flew to Wausau to meet with a Mosinee director, the corporation's comptroller and its general counsel. Hall counseled that a stock split and a rapid increase in cash dividends would be effective antitakeover techniques. The meeting ended with management's decision to bring the matters before the board at its regular meeting, scheduled for December 22.

A few days later, on December 14, Hall purchased 1,000 shares of Mosinee common at an average price of $17 a share. Unaware of his holdings in the company, Mosinee executives continued to discuss their stock and cash-dividend proposals with Hall, seeking, among other things, his opinion on the optimum amount of such dividends. In a classic conflict of interest, the corporate counselor was in position to enrich himself.

On December 20 Hall learned through his management contacts (including the corporation's chairman) that at its forthcoming December 22 meeting the board would consider—and would likely approve—a sizable stock dividend and a substantial increase in the cash dividend. Acting on this inside information, the trusted attorney purchased an additional 900 Mosinee shares on December 20, at an average price of $17.50 per share. Later that day Hall spoke with Mosinee's general counsel on the subjects of stock and cash dividends. In this conversation, which came fewer than eight hours after his purchase of Mosinee stock, Hall counseled in favor of a stock dividend and an increased cash dividend.

The payoff for this behind-the-scenes activity was just around the corner. On December 22 the board acted just as Hall had expected, approving a two-for-one stock dividend and a 33⅓ percent increase in regular quarterly cash dividends. A day later, the stock climbed to $19.75 a share. As the court papers later stated, "During the period of Hall's service as attorney and legal adviser for Mosinee, Hall would and did provide legal counsel and advice to the directors, officers, attorneys and fiduciaries of Mosinee while concealing that as a recent undisclosed purchaser of Mosinee's stock, Hall would derive personal gain and benefit from a stock or cash dividend."

But there would be more and bigger purchases ahead for Mr. Hall. On January 8, 1979, he would learn that another longtime client, Kansas City Southern Industries, a holding company for Kansas City Southern Railway and other diversified enterprises, was considering an acquisition of Pioneer Western, an insurance company. Hall was advised that the prospective acquisition— which had already been discussed with Pioneer—would involve the payment of a substantial cash premium to Pioneer. As part of his marching orders, Hall was instructed to retain local counsel in three states—Missouri, Florida and Ohio—whose takeover and insurance statutes were applicable to the proposed acquisition.

In a letter dated January 10, 1979, from his client Kansas City Southern Industries, Hall received a draft chronology of the steps necessary to acquire Pioneer and a proposed letter to Pioneer's major shareholders. Included in this document—which served as a blueprint for the takeover—was a recommendation that KCSI offer Pioneer shareholders $16 for each share of Pioneer common stock, a good deal more than its over-the-counter bid price of $11.25.

On January 15 and 16 Hall had numerous telephone conversations with KCSI officials (including the company's president), in which he informed them of favorable reports from local counsel and discussed various tactics for the takeover. Convinced that the deal would proceed, Hall purchased 2,000 shares of Pioneer common on January 17 at $11.75 per share.

Less than a week later Hall was back in Kansas City to attend a meeting at KCSI offices concerning the Pioneer acquisition. Here he picked up another valuable tidbit. Having just concluded a banner year, his client had racked up a 60-percent increase in net earnings. Taking this still confidential news directly to market, Hall purchased 500 shares of KCSI's common stock at $20 per share. Soon after, the stock rose to $22 a share on news of the increased earnings.

On the acquisition front, KCSI and Pioneer issued a joint press release on February 20, announcing that they had reached an agreement in principle, under which KCSI would offer $17 a share for all of the outstanding shares of Pioneer common stock. The following day, Pioneer stock traded at about $15.50 and KCSI closed at $23. After the remaining details were ironed out, KCSI announced on April 6 that it would proceed with the $17-a-share tender offer on April 11. Hall had only to wait for the best time to sell. That came on April 9, when Pioneer stock hit $16⅝. When his costs were subtracted, the New York lawyer counted a net profit of $9,176.51 on the Pioneer shares alone.

The Pioneer deal represented an expansion in Hall's insider transactions. Now he was dabbling in two client stocks simultaneously. As with all inside traders—Boesky, Levine, Wilkis, Tome—his greed fed on itself.

Hall's second front opened when he was hired in March 1979 by Conchemo, Inc., a Lenaxa, Kansas–based manufacturer of mobile homes and other products. Conchemo was listed on the American Stock Exchange. Having just completed a sale of its coatings division for $15 million, Conchemo found that it would have net cash reserves of $21 million. Wanting to put the cash to work, management pondered four alternatives: expansion of its remaining divisions; acquisition of other businesses; repurchase of its own stock through a tender offer; or a dividend to its shareholders. After much internal deliberation, a tender offer by the company for its own securities emerged as the most viable choice. Dave Hall was contacted to discuss the transaction.

On March 26 Hall met with representatives of Conchemo management and with the corporation's financial adviser to discuss the terms of the proposed tender. As the plan took shape, Conchemo would make an offer for its common stock at a price substantially higher than the current market quote of $16.50 per share. The proposal would be submitted to Conchemo's board of directors on April 5 and, if approved, would commence on April 10.

As scheduled, the board met on April 5, deciding in favor of tendering for up to 400,000 shares, or 41 percent of Conchemo's outstanding common stock, at a price of between $24 and $28 per share. But formal authorization was withheld until the board could obtain outside confirmation of the fairness of the tender-offer price. Under the revised plan, this would be obtained by the next board meeting, scheduled for April 16, with the tender delayed until April 17. Hall, who attended the April 5 board meeting, was privy to Conchemo's plans—none of which was announced to the public.

Hall soon received draft copies of Conchemo's proposed tender-offer materials—almost a guarantee that the corporation would proceed with its stock repurchase plan. Convinced that he'd latched onto a sure thing, attorney Hall acted the same day, buying 2,000 shares of his client's stock at an average price of $19.50 per share.

Less than twenty-four hours later, Hall flew to Kansas City to review the still "secret" tender-offer materials with Conchemo's management and to prepare them for printing. With all the kinks ironed out, the documents were mailed to the printer on April 11. The next day, Hall went back to the market, gobbling up another 1,000 Conchemo shares at an average price of $21 each.

But he didn't stop there. On Monday morning, April 16, Hall returned to Kansas City to attend what would be the final board meeting before the tender was launched. But before leaving Kansas City airport on his way to Conchemo's offices, Hall, apparently struck by the opportunity before him, telephoned his New York broker, ordering another 2,000 shares of his client's stock. The order was executed a few minutes later at an average price of $21.25 per share.

It was, as with the previous purchases, a virtually riskless investment. Within hours Conchemo's board formally authorized the tender offer at $27 per share. The news was made public at approximately five in the afternoon. The next day Conchemo stock soared 5 points to $26. On April 18 Hall sold 1,000 shares at that price, for a profit of $6,500, based on his initial purchases.

The damage in the Hall case was limited by the fact that he was a small practitioner operating solely for his own benefit. But when a large law firm is involved—and most big M&A deals are handled by legal behemoths with 300 to 750 lawyers—the opportunity for widespread leaks and for pervasive insider trading is compounded exponentially.

Such was the case in 1983 when underlings in the administrative staff broke the internal code on pending takeovers at New York's Skadden Arps Slate Meagher & Flom, the nation's premier M&A law firm, whose senior partner Joseph Flom worked alongside Dave Hall's former partner George Demas in the corporate proxy battles of the fifties and sixties. The Skadden Arps staffers fed the information to a network of accomplices including stockbrokers and a Brooklyn-based cab driver.

The episode captures the problem of insider trading in microcosm, revealing that the bureaucracy of advisers brought in on mergers and acquisitions has become so extensive that confidentiality is next to impossible. If the principals don't break the rules, their subordinates will. The sheer mass of confidential information is simply too great to control. Measures to prevent it from slipping out, such as boilerplate rules against insider trading at Skadden Arps, are akin to piling sandbags against a tidal wave.

According to the SEC, the scheme (which turned out to be a two-headed monster) began when Alfred Salvatore, a proofreader in the Skadden Arps back office, struck a deal to pass confidential information on pending corporate mergers, takeovers and buyouts to his friend, stockbroker Aaron Lerman. Needing help to carry out his side of the bargain, Salvatore enlisted Steven Crow, a supervisor in the firm's word-processing department. Lerman, in turn, allegedly agreed to sell what he would learn to a fellow stockbroker, Prudential-Bache Securities colleague Stephen Karanzalis.

As the scheme unfolded, the Skadden Arps insiders would use their access to the law firm's classified computer files to sniff out news of pending takeovers and then pass it on to the brokers, who would use it for personal gain. In return for their critical role as the inside men passing along client secrets, Crow and Salvatore—clearly nickel-and-dime players in the underworld of inside traders—would receive cash payments.

It all seemed so easy. Picking up on the office grapevine, Crow and Salvatore would identify attorneys working on M&A deals and would rifle through their letters and documents stored in the Skadden Arps computer. Although passwords were required for entry into the files, the men had learned many of them through their official functions at the firm.

Armed with these keys to the vault, the duo uncovered a wealth of information that led, through the broker connection, to a trading spree. In a typical case, Skadden Arps represented Coastal Corporation in its tender offer for Texas Gas Resources. Learning of the deal about a month before it was announced in June 1983, the Skadden Arps tippers passed word to the brokers. Between May 16 and May 19 Karanzalis bought 8,000 shares of the stock for seventeen of his Prudential-Bache accounts. Included in those accounts were Karanzalis's wife, friends of Lerman and another stockbroker with E. F. Hutton, who in turn bought 13,250 shares for his accounts.

Later that year, Skadden Arps counseled Calvin Klein, Inc., in its tender offer for Puritan Fashions. As the background legal work progressed from July to November, Karanzalis bought 29,700 Puritan shares for seven of his accounts, including one he shared with his wife, one for another relative and one for the wife of one of Lerman's associates.

Another tip led to trades in Houston Natural Gas in advance of a tender offer by Coastal Corporation. In this transaction, which illustrates just how inside information literally hemorrhages through a thousand leaks, Dennis Levine also learned of the acquisition from his trading accomplice Robert Wilkis, whose firm, Lazard Frères, was representing Houston Natural Gas. Levine, in turn, whispered what he knew to Ivan Boesky. Levine bought 74,800 shares; Boesky went for 301,800.

Chances are good the Skadden Arps ring would have avoided detection for years, had it not been for a informant who contacted the SEC and the New York Stock Exchange, charging that something was foul in the prestigious law firm. With the Big Board and the SEC already exploring preannouncement trading surges in some of the stocks but unable to trace a source of leaks, the lead on Skadden Arps was the missing puzzle piece.

"We took what we knew to Skadden's management, which cooperated fully from the start," says SEC trial attorney Robert Blackburn, who handled the case for the government. "They hired a private investigator who cooperated with us in finding out who was responsible for the leaks.

"It didn't take long to narrow it down to a few candidates in the administrative area. They were the only ones who had access to all of the information that was leaking out. When we looked at the deals involved, we found that no one lawyer worked on all of them. If there were four cases, we'd find that lawyer A worked on cases one and two but not three and four, while lawyer B worked on three and four but not one and two. But some of the administrative people had access to documents for all the cases."

With the investigation narrowed down to a small band of suspects, the private eyes got the kind of breaks in the case normally reserved for Perry Mason. Working in what he thought were deserted offices, Crow—the word-processing department's night-shift manager—programmed the computer to seek all references with dollar signs, checking each entry for evidence of takeovers. A perfect crime, or so he thought. But little did he know that a superior, alerted to shadow the twenty-nine-year-old Crow, was secretly watching him at work, monitoring his computer screen to see which documents he was calling up. It was clear from his choice of material that the word processor was scavenging for confidential information.

Crow's former boss stated: "On two occasions during March 1984, unknown to Mr. Crow, I personally observed Mr. Crow scanning the contents of numerous confidential documents stored in the Skadden Arps ATEX system, which documents had been prepared by several attorneys employed by Skadden Arps and which contained confidential information about proposed business combinations and corporate securities transactions with respect to numerous Skadden Arps clients; for example, stock purchase agreements, and drafts of offers to purchase stock, beneficial ownership documents as well as other legal documents which I understand are essential to business combinations and corporate securities acquisitions. Most of the documents I observed Mr. Crow accessing were matters he was not assigned to work on and which he had no legitimate purpose reviewing. These documents related to confidential client matters with respect to, among others, Midlands and Two Company. On at least one occasion, Mr. Crow reviewed documents solely to identify all references to dollar figures."

But this alone did not prove insider trading. To make a strong case, proof was needed of an outside connection. One or several parties had to be caught basing stock market activities on confidential information in Skadden Arps client files. This connection came in a one-in-a-million strike. The law firm's private eyes had expanded their surveillance of the suspects to their off-work hours. They watched from a distance as one of them dumped a bag of garbage into a bin outside of his apartment building. Retrieving the refuse on a hunch, the investigators hit pay dirt. Stuffed in Chinese food containers, still coated with black bean sauce and bits of egg roll, were handwritten notes referring to "Mr. Inside" and "Mr. Outside" and information on pending client deals.

On another front, surveillance of Lerman revealed a connection with Karanzalis and Salvatore. A private investigator for Skadden Arps reported: "On Sunday, March 11, 1984, I was conducting surveillance outside of Lerman's residence. At 1:55 P.M., Salvatore entered the building, and left again at about 7:08 P.M. I understand that later that evening, Michael Kohut, an investigator with whom I was conducting surveillance that day and who continued surveillance after I left that evening, saw a man arrive by car at Lerman's residence and enter the building. Kohut noted the car's license plate number. I further understand from conversations with personnel associated with my firm that a check of the license plate number revealed that the car was registered to Patricia Karanzalis. The motor vehicle records note that Ms. Karanzalis owns the car jointly with her husband."

Convinced that they had developed a mainline of information to outside sources, the SEC called in the U.S. Attorney's Office for the Southern District of New York. Launching a preemptive strike against the suspects, the Feds, who had obtained arrest and search warrants, burst into the Skadden Arps offices, collaring Crow and Salvatore on the spot. Finding themselves frisked and handcuffed by armed marshals, the two back-office functionaries spilled the beans on their accomplices and, in a connection that surprised the SEC and the U.S. Attorney's Office, told of another secret trading operation thriving under the Skadden Arps roof.

According to the SEC, this one began in 1982 when Stephen Wallis, a thirty-year-old driver with New York City's Dial-a-Cab, picked up Skadden Arps proofreader Kenneth Petricig, a support staffer whose job gave him access to sensitive legal documents. To Wallis, a self-taught expert on foreign secrecy laws who had long dreamed of striking it rich, his precious cargo represented an opportunity to eavesdrop on valuable corporate secrets. Knowing that Skadden Arps advised dozens of corporations, takeover artists and investment banks and that the firm's word processors were studded with the identities of suitors, targets and white knights, Wallis proposed a deal: Petricig would pass him information in return for cash payments.

"Apparently they had worked out quite a sophisticated scheme," Blackburn says. "For example, when Petricig wanted to contact Wallis, he'd place a call to a paging service that would then buzz Wallis on a portable beeper. To avoid having his calls traced, Petricig would place them from a rotating series of pay telephones and would leave messages in numeric codes the two men had worked out together. The number 'one' might mean that Petricig had information for Wallis, 'two' might mean they should get together, and 'three' might signal that a problem had developed and they should not be seen together."

In time, Petricig, Crow and Salvatore learned that they were up to similar activities, and they began to share information for the benefit of their outside clients. On the basis of leaks from one or all of these sources, which were always relayed to him by Petricig, Wallis made the following investments:

- On May 16, 1983, he purchased (in a joint account he maintained with his girlfriend, Sharon Willey) 3,000 shares of Texas Gas Resources for a total cost of about $92,400.

- Between August 15 and October 5, 1983, he bought 16,000 shares of Puritan for a total cost of more than $300,000.

- Beginning November 4, 1983, he acquired 2,400 shares of Houston Natural Gas for a total cost of over $117,000. He also bought thirty call options for a cost exceeding $36,000 and, in an account with his girlfriend, bought 211 Houston Natural Gas options, representing the right to buy 21,100 common shares at a fixed price. Starting in January 1984, his girlfriend gobbled up 400 Houston Natural Gas shares for her own account.

- Beginning in March 1984, he bought 500 shares of Midlands Energy, which was sought after by a Skadden Arps client, Evmar, for a leveraged buyout or other business combination.

- Also in March 1984, he took a 3,000-share stake in Southwest Forest Industries, which was under consideration by another Skadden Arps client for a leveraged buyout. Another 7,500 shares were purchased for the joint account with Wallis's girlfriend.

- Additional trades were made in the stocks of General American Oil Corporation, the subject of a possible takeover by Skadden Arps client Mesa Petroleum; of Northwest Energy, pursued by The Williams Companies, another Skadden Arps client; and of Maryland Cup Corporation, the target of Fort Howard Paper Company. (Dennis Levine also took a 15,200-share stake in this one, learning of the transaction through his capacity as an investment banker with Lehman Brothers, which represented Maryland Cup.)

But the roof of the trading scheme caved in when Petricig, fingered by his co-workers Crow and Salvatore, agreed to cooperate with the Feds by wearing a wire at his next meeting with Wallis. It was here that the cabbie, who prided himself on his knowledge of the securities laws and how to evade them, sealed his own fate.

"Not knowing that he was being taped, Wallis bragged about how airtight his system was, how he had set up Swiss bank accounts to evade detection by the authorities and how he would never get caught," Blackburn says. "If there was ever a case of a guy putting his foot in his mouth, this was it.

"Not only was the tape damaging evidence, but when the government searched Wallis's home, they found notes, files and documents on the law firm's activities and on Wallis's relationship with Petricig. Although Wallis and Willey tried at first to fight us—contesting a motion for a preliminary injunction—they soon recognized how strong our case was and settled with us and the U.S. Attorney's Office."

When the dust cleared, the members of the Skadden Arps ring found themselves faced with the following sentences:

- Crow, Salvatore and Petricig: three years on probation; restitution; 150 hours of community service for each year of probation

- Willey: five years on probation; $34,000 restitution

- Wallis: weekends in prison for eighteen months; five years on probation; $49,000 restitution

- Lerman: six months' imprisonment; four years on probation; 200 hours of community service

- Karanzalis, who settled with the SEC, agreed to repay $36,000 and was barred from working for brokers or investments firms

The case illustrates that though corporate law firms may have controls designed to discourage employees from leaking confidential information, these often aren't worth the paper they're printed on. Crow, Salvatore and Petricig all signed acknowledgments that they had received, read and understood Skadden Arps' Confidentiality and Security Investments Policy, which stated that "information that a client intends to make or assist in making a tender offer for a particular target company would bar firm personnel from trading in the target company's securities, as well as in the offeror's, and from 'tipping' others about the plan."

When money was flashed before their eyes, inside traders at Skadden Arps ignored the pledge as if they had never seen it. The chance to profit from the new gold rush—mergers and acquisitions—proved too tempting to pass up.

But how did this fever spread to Wall Street's old-line law firms?

Once viewed as the bailiwick of corporate ambulance chasers, merger-and-acquisition practice gained acceptability at Wall Street's white-shoe law firms only after aggressive upstarts like Skadden Arps and its archrival, Wachtell, Lipton, Rosen & Katz, carved out a burgeoning market where others once feared to tread. With Skadden emerging as the most profitable law firm in the nation, primarily because of Joe Flom's merger-and-acquisition practice, and with Wachtell, Lipton partners becoming the richest in the profession, with incomes of $1 million and more a year, other firms that had dismissed M&A as a sloppy, short-lived business started posturing for a piece of the action.

Since the late seventies and early eighties, virtually all of the time-warped legal institutions—many of which had grown fat and listless along with the staid banking and securities clients that had enriched them for a century or more—moved en masse to cultivate M&A clients. Most have stumbled into the market, ill prepared for the special security problems that go hand in hand with advance information on corporate restructurings. While there has always been a need to protect client confidences, the hunger for this information and the ability to turn it into quick profits were rare before the firms found themselves knee-deep in takeover practice. Suddenly a chain of partners and associates, as well as proofreaders, clerks and secretaries, has access to the kind of corporate intelligence that could make them rich.

Generally, word of emerging takeovers comes to the law firms at the highest levels. In a typical episode, the Wall Street law firm of Sullivan & Cromwell learned in the spring of 1985 that a shark was circling the waters around longtime client Kaiser Aluminum & Chemical Corporation. A 108-year-old elitist partnership that had made a 180-degree about-face on takeover practice when it set up an M&A unit in 1978, Sullivan & Cromwell has fared well at the game, inheriting a full plate of work from its investment banking clients Goldman Sachs and Morgan Stanley. So when partner John Merow, a member of Kaiser's board of directors, informed his colleagues at the firm that someone was nibbling at the client's stock, they found themselves in familiar territory.

It seemed that Joseph Frates III, a Tulsa-based investor with a penchant for acquiring undervalued companies, had called Kaiser's chairman, Cornell Maier, and invited himself in for a talk. Given Frates's track record, Maier knew that he had more on his mind than a tour of the offices. Clearly he was interested in buying the company.

"Frates and a group he worked with had already acquired Kaiser Steel and flipped it for a quick profit," says Benjamin Stapleton, a Sullivan & Cromwell M&A partner, and one of the first to learn of the potential play for Kaiser Aluminum. "We considered it a good bet that Frates had visions of doing the same with the aluminum company."

At this time, Frates's interest in meeting with Kaiser—which was known only to the lawyers and a select group of insiders—could bode well for its stock price. With Kaiser suffering through a dismal period in which its stock languished at about $12 a share, news that a shark was considering a play for the company would be an invaluable element from an investment standpoint and a ray of bullishness in a very bearish period. This was good reason to buy the stock, but a reason only the insiders knew.

For Kaiser management, the critical question was just how to deal with Frates. Here the lawyers, as principal advisers, helped shape the company's policy. Inviting the prospective shark into their midst, they counseled, could signal that they were interested in cutting some kind of deal. The signal in this case would be misleading. With Kaiser stock selling at a low point, and with management convinced that a turnaround was in the offing, selling to Frates at this time would be playing into his hands—allowing him, in effect, to walk away with the bargain of a lifetime.

But with a great bulk of Kaiser's stock held by institutional investors a good deal more sophisticated than the average mom and pop stockholder, management could not appear out of touch with the shareholders' interests. Were the impression to get out that Kaiser was uninterested in a deal at any price, that management's only objective was to save itself, the institutions that had so far remained loyal might lean toward Frates.

With the lawyers laying out both sides of the issue, Kaiser decided at first to meet with Frates, allowing him to state his position. But this position, according to Stapleton, a Yale Law School alumnus who started with Sullivan & Cromwell in 1969, was not very clear:

"Frates was always somewhat vague about his plans. Basically, he wanted to buy a big position, do some sort of leveraged transaction, sell some assets, pay down debt and maybe flip the company to somebody else."

But to Frates, a shrewd investor who first became famous for buying and then reselling the LBJ Ranch to the Johnson family, it was simply a matter of getting more value for the troubled company's shareholders.

After numerous back-and-forths between the company and Frates, Kaiser management made it clear to the potential acquirer that it was not interested in selling. Frates, who at this point controlled only a small amount of Kaiser stock, responded that Kaiser hadn't heard the last of him and went in search of allies. He surfaced with a 13-D filing that indicated that, along with the arbitrage firm Jamie Securities, he controlled 5 percent of the outstanding shares. Still a small player, he was viewed with concern but not any kind of panic by Kaiser management or by Sullivan & Cromwell, which was orchestrating the takeover defense. Still, to keep him off balance, the lawyers filed a suit against the investor group, claiming their 13-D filing was false and misleading.

The takeover threat turned more ominous in the latter part of 1985, as the Frates group teamed up with Alan Clore, a wealthy investor involved in a number of previous takeovers. With this new money, the group started accumulating Kaiser stock at an aggressive pace, claiming 20 percent of the outstanding shares by January 1986. It was then that the invaders tried to gain control of the company by replacing the board of directors with their own slate of candidates. Under a so-called "consent" procedure allowed under the laws of Delaware, where Kaiser was incorporated, they sought to achieve their goal by getting 50 percent of the stockholders to sign consent forms approving the shakeup.

"But they failed at this, and at a subsequent effort to take control at our annual meeting, because we were able to convince the institutions that the deal the prospective acquirers were offering was more to their own benefit than anyone else's," Stapleton says. "In the end, the institutions stuck with us. Management and the board retained control of the company."

Later in the year a deal would be cut between Kaiser and Clore, giving the investor's group control of the board while allowing corporate management to remain in place.

But by the time the acquirers made their move at the annual meeting, Kaiser's stock had risen to $21.50, about $7 a share more than when Frates first contacted management—and management, in turn, contacted its lawyers. Although the rise was due in part to favorable analyst reports concerning Kaiser's turnaround prospects, much of the rise was attributable to early rumors of a takeover (before the 13-D was filed) and the investor group's attempts to acquire the company. Had any of the lawyers or, for that matter, Kaiser's investment bankers, Drexel Burnham Lambert, purchased Kaiser stock at the outset, they would have made a killing on the run-up in the shares.

Although there is no evidence that individuals at Sullivan & Cromwell or Drexel Burnham traded on the stock, the firms' internal controls are less than impressive. Here again, management relies on the consistently unreliable "trust" factor.

"If you invest in the stock of a client, you are supposed to clear it with the partner in charge of that client," Stapleton says. "But clearly none of us invests in any of the takeover situations. There's probably something in our office manual on this, but I think it's so absolutely clear that . . . it wouldn't happen."

Wouldn't happen? Stapleton may have been referring to the firm's professional staff—trusting that the learned barristers of Sullivan & Cromwell wouldn't succumb to the same temptations as Dave Hall, Ilan Reich or Michael David. But leaks can spring from a hundred sources, from people who have no legal degrees on their walls—a fact that Stapleton and the entire Sullivan & Cromwell partnership are painfully aware of. Mention the name Alan Ihne and they wince in unison. The firm's former office manager, Ihne leaked information from secret client documents to a trading ring that included up to fifteen participants. The scheme brought him a sentence of up to three and a half years in prison.

As we have learned, Ihne was not an isolated case. Since 1980 the U.S. Attorney's Office for the Southern District of New York has prosecuted a broad cross-section of law-firm employees including attorneys, computer processors, proofreaders, an office manager, an accounting clerk and a purchasing manager. The list of firms tainted by these scandals includes the most prominent names in M&A and general corporate law: Skadden Arps; Wachtell, Lipton; Fried, Frank; Sullivan & Cromwell; Paul, Weiss.

Were an attorney presenting a case to a jury, he would have to say the evidence is overwhelming: takeover practice is a corrupting influence on law firms. When there is the opportunity to turn corporate secrets into cash, rules and laws and ethics are "meant to be broken."

Admits Sullivan & Cromwell's Stapleton: "I don't think it [insider trading] can ever be stopped completely cold. There's a lot of money to be made very quickly and a lot of people are shortsighted and greedy."

VIII

The Early Returns

"Pay your employees so little that they can't afford to invest in the market, no matter what they learn. Other than that, nothing will work. And even that has loopholes. They can always borrow from their uncles."

—*A major proxy solicitor's tongue-in-cheek solution for curbing insider trading*

In the pretzel logic of inside trading laws, gaining secret information from insiders such as lawyers, bankers or arbs is illegal; uncovering it on your own is ingenious. The former makes you a criminal; the latter makes you rich.

With this in mind, an extensive Wall Street subculture has emerged, its principal function being the discovery of corporate secrets—ostensibly through legal means—before the investment community and subsequently the general public catch on. These professional snoops, including legitimate arbs and another group called stock watchers, create a gray area in which lawbreakers can hide, shielded as they are by a cloak of professionalism. Was a string of timely investments made on the basis of sound detective work as these professionals insist, or was it, as the SEC often believes, based on a secret call from a corporate informer? With scores of Wall Streeters virtually licensed to ferret out corporate secrets and strategies, foul play can be difficult to prove.

Among the first to spot a takeover in the making, for example, is a group of functionaries who spend their days fixed before a bank of computer terminals waiting for bells to ring, alarms to blare. Housed in a small, airless room on the thirtieth floor of One Wall Street Plaza (the corner of Maiden Lane and Water Street) the Georgeson Stock Watchers are wired electronically and by telephone into all major stock exchanges, brokerage houses, investment banks and the arbitrage community. Their job: to spot the early warning signs of a hostile takeover and flash the word to the target company days or hours before the news is public. It is financial sleuthing, high-tech style. Consider this case:

"We were doing routine surveillance of a client company's stock—looking for any and all trading anomalies—when we noticed that a major broker had started accumulating the shares," says Richard Wines, a polite but formal man who runs the Stock Watch program for the venerable proxy house of Georgeson & Company. Other Wall Street proxy firms have similar services.

"Something to be concerned about? Maybe, maybe not. The accumulation could be nothing more than an institutional investor buying the shares for its portfolio. Perhaps the fund manager liked the stock and was buying it as a routine investment. Perfectly innocent, or was it? That explanation became less plausible when a major bank started accumulating the stock, and then in the following weeks a second commercial bank and an investment bank started taking big positions in it.

"Was this a series of unrelated purchases? Clearly, somebody wanted it to look that way, but our analysis of the accumulations indicated a raider at work. By assembling a number of puzzle pieces, including our knowledge of the banks involved—some Canadian banks and some Canadian banks piggybacking on American banks—and their major customers, we soon narrowed this down further, identifying the sharks as the Belzberg family of Canada.

"The Belzbergs had timed their move well, making a run just when the target company was the focus of intensive news coverage having nothing to do with a stock takeover. Media interest spurs trading in a company's stock, providing a natural camouflage for the raiders' attack. When the price and volume rise, the market writes this off to the news story rather than to the developing, but still secret, takeover."

That's likely what the Belzbergs—a tight-lipped clan of Canadian entrepreneurs grown infamous for their pursuit of corporate prey—had in mind. And for a while their strategy worked, hoodwinking virtually everyone on the Street but Georgeson's Stock Watchers. Why this financial SWAT team was able to see through the ruse has as much to do with their position as insiders as with their skill in uncovering market manipulations.

The fact is, the Georgeson insiders knew about the Belzbergs before most of the arbitragers, before the investment bankers, before anyone else except the Belzberg team, because they were privy to the target company's depositary records. This information, culled from the four major depositaries that store stock certificates, shows which banks and brokers are holding how many of the company's shares. For example, if investor A buys 100,000 shares of Pan Am through E. F. Hutton, the records at Depositary Trust Company in New York will reveal that 100,000 Pan Am shares have settled in Hutton's account. Should A wind up selling, and B, a Merrill Lynch customer, wind up buying, the 100,000 shares will be seen moving out of Hutton's depositary accounts and into those of Merrill Lynch.

Because Georgeson is authorized by the Stock Watch client to review depositary records and thus to track stock movements, it gains access to what is otherwise proprietary information. Blessed with this data—what Guy Wyser-Pratte calls "the perfect knowledge"—Stock Watch analysts can monitor changes in stock holdings from one institution to another that the rest of the market is oblivious to and can then use this intelligence to decipher secret corporate activities, all of which is legal.

In a typical case, Wines noticed trading anomalies in a client's stock as shares seesawed back and forth from one broker to another and at times to a suspicious account at the First National Bank of Minneapolis, an institution patronized by takeover artist Irwin Jacobs. What was going on? Why were the shares suddenly moving in this strange pattern? Was this the work of a haphazard investor or was it a diversionary tactic designed to shift attention from the investor's real objectives? As Wines probed deeper, he saw the signature of one of Wall Street's most devious operatives.

"Judging from the trading pattern, we deduced that many of the purchases were being made by Ivan Boesky. In a rare practice for him, he was leaving part of his trail exposed, intentionally so. Why? Because he wanted it to look like he was selling the shares when he was really just shifting them from one of his accounts to another. He wanted to maintain a large position in the shares without anyone knowing about it.

"Our client was duped by his strategy. When they looked at their depositary lists and saw that Boesky had relinquished his shares, they said, 'Ah good, Boesky's out.' But we showed them that wasn't really the case—that Boesky wasn't really out. Instead of selling, he was just moving the stock around in a sophisticated version of the old shell game.

"Boesky's gambit was built around a dizzying series of stock transfers whereby the arb loaned shares to a brokerage firm that in turn loaned them to another broker, who ultimately used them to cover short positions. We saw through this by discovering a pattern of increases and decreases in the depositary positions of the three separate accounts. Whenever there was an increase in one, there was a decrease in the other two, and so on."

Because these were private rather than market transactions, conducted from seller to buyer outside of the stock exchanges, Georgeson had an advantage in detecting them. As ordained insiders, people at Georgeson were the only ones with the client company's depositary records. Combined with their skill in piecing together market transactions, that could give them a valuable edge for spotting takeovers in the making, which is precisely why client companies have been flocking to stock-watch services in record numbers. With corporate raiders circling the waters like starved piranhas, CEOs see round-the-clock surveillance of their company's stock as a first line of defense against surprise attacks. Should the raider be planning a takeover, or should he be putting the wheels in motion by accumulating shares, management wants enough lead time to ward off the attack. At Georgeson, Stock Watch fills the bill by serving as an early warning system against hostile assaults.

Stock Watchers begin their surveillance by monitoring a stock's normal trading range (in price per share and volume of shares) for the past quarter and full year. This pattern, which is entered in Stock Watch computers, establishes the parameters within which the stock can trade without giving evidence of unusual market activities. Should trading cross any of the established thresholds, alarms built into the Stock Watch software go off, alerting the analysts to investigate further. When such obvious explanations as a favorable brokerage report or a major purchase by a mutual fund fail to explain a sudden run-up in price or volume, the Georgeson team races to the phones, jumping all over a network of sources including brokers, investment bankers and arbs.

Learning to tell who has insight and who just wants to move his lips is important here. "Wall Street sources never admit they don't know what's happening," Wines says, "so you have to learn to tell when they're guessing and when they really know what's behind the trading anomalies. It's an instinct you develop."

Should all sources turn up dry, the search goes into high gear, with Stock Watchers checking the depositary listings to see where the stock is settling after the market trading. But there's still a missing link. Valuable as they are, depositary records fail to reveal the stock's "beneficial owners"—the individuals or institutions for whom the banks and brokers are holding the shares. Filling in that blank always takes a bit of Sherlock Holmesing and is especially tricky in the earliest stages of a takeover, when the shark is determined to acquire shares without tipping the market to his plan. He is building significant accumulations, yes, but under cover of a bank or broker. At this point, the buyer's identity is not known. The corporation and the market in general are in the dark. Is it a passive investor, simply building positions in a favored stock? Is it a greenmailer acquiring his ransom for a takeover threat? Or is it an equity-eating shark seeking to control the company?

Getting the answer—and getting it swiftly—is critical to the hand-wringing CEO. Should the buyer turn out to be a Saul Steinberg, an Irwin Jacobs or a T. Boone Pickens, chances are good the initial purchases are but a prelude to a full-scale assault. Knowing who's pulling the strings offers a revealing glimpse of what's likely to follow. Here again, the Stock Watchers have an advantage. It stems from Georgeson's primary role as one of Wall Street's three major proxy solicitors.

"We gain valuable clues from our proxy solicitation campaigns," Georgeson vice-president Ray Lewis explains. "For example, when the proxies are voted, they're usually identified by an account number only. In most cases, you can't identify the beneficial owner by name. But now and then the vote comes in with a name and return address on the envelope. In effect the stockholder identifies himself. Whether that's inadvertent or not, a relationship between that name and account number is permanently stored in our computers. When the same account number surfaces again in a future transaction—this time without a name on the envelope—the computer remembers the association between the number and the name and alerts us to it. So when a client asks who's behind the heavy surge of buying in its stock, we can say, 'That's so-and-so, the corporate raider.'"

Clients aren't the only ones who covet that information. When the phone rings at Georgeson, odds are there's an arbitrager on the other end. Blessed with its top-secret arsenal of depositary transfers and proxy data, Georgeson holds puzzle pieces that the arbs, who earn their fortunes sniffing out takeovers before they make the front page of *The Wall Street Journal*, would dearly love to have. But this is a two-way street, with the stock watchers seeking information from the arbs as well. The truth is that everyone in the M&A business—whether as detective, investor or adviser—is wired into everyone else. The notion of a pristine group of insiders roped off in a soundproof isolation booth is about as far from the real world as an MBA course on business ethics. Although the stock-watch firms prefer to tout their in-house expertise, their sexy computer programs and proprietary stock records, there's no doubt that they still look to the Wall Street rumor mill for critical clues on takeovers in the making.

Given Wall Street's "you scratch my back, I'll scratch yours" attitude, are the stock watchers tempted to reveal inside information to gain cooperation from powerful arbs like Ivan Boesky? Are they inclined to trade depositary data for news the arbs have picked up from their own networks of lawyers, bankers and Dennis Levines of the Street?

While the Georgeson people admit to "idle chatter" with the arbs, they deny that privileged information ever passes from their lips, holding that everything proprietary stays within One Wall Street Plaza. Why then do the arbs (never really known for "idle chatter") bother to call? Asked about this, the Georgeson Stock Watchers turn the question around, hinting about when and why they call the arbs, but not to why the arbs return the favor. A Georgeson executive puts it this way: "We would generally talk to an arb when there is anomalous trading going on. Something the arbs already know about. We are obviously not going to trade inside information with them.

"What can we tell them? We can tell them, hey look, X stock is trading wildly today. What do you know about it? What's going on? What are the rumors? That kind of thing."

While there is no evidence that information leaks from this or any of the stock-watch services, the opportunities for leakage are as plentiful as tips on Wall Street, and stock watchers are uncharacteristically glib on what the arbs want to know and on what they are told.

Georgeson's description of its relationship with the arbs does not fit the facts on how the Street operates. The arbs don't need the stock watchers to tell them that "X stock is trading wildly today." With their eyes cemented to Quotrons the size of Panavision screens, arbs know of trading activity the instant it occurs—if not sooner. And if they can answer Georgeson's questions "What's going on? What are the rumors?" will they tell all simply to make life easier for Georgeson and its clients? Or will they expect in return, in this world of reciprocal back-scratching, takeover intelligence they can't find on the Dow Jones wire? The answer depends on one's view of Wall Street. Is it motivated by collegiality or, as the Dennis Levine and Ivan Boesky cases indicate, by greed and power?

The question applies to stock-watch staffers, many of whom are faced with enormous temptations. While takeover artists must file with the SEC once they have acquired 5 percent of a corporation's stock—thus making their purchases (and perhaps their ultimate intentions) public—Georgeson claims that its Stock Watch sleuths can identify accumulations well before this, ringing the alarm when the buyer and prospective acquirer have as little as one-half percent of the outstanding shares. The firm's batting average in sniffing out takeovers in the making is said to be better than 85 percent.

If they were to use the information for inside trading, that kind of performance could make stock-watch analysts rich enough to warrant Swiss accounts of their own. With this in mind, Georgeson has installed internal controls designed, ostensibly, to prevent employees from profiting on inside information or from passing the word to friends, relatives, business associates, elevator operators and so forth.

But are the controls effective? The answer is yes and no. Yes, Georgeson forbids employees from sharing secret data with outsiders and from trading in the stocks of client companies without prior approval of top management. But no, it doesn't check on compliance, and no, it does little to enforce its ban on misusing information. Georgeson's compliance program—so similar to that of the other key M&A players it seems to be bought off the rack—appears to be window dressing. Asked if the firm bans insider trading, management says "of course" and points to the company's rules. But does Georgeson audit its employees' brokerage accounts? No. Does it require that staffers trade through a central account? No. Does it make a serious effort to catch would-be offenders? Perhaps, but in Georgeson's fifty-year history as a proxy solicitor, exposed as it has been to a vault full of inside information, not a single employee has ever been caught engaging in insider trading.

"We know our employees, we choose them carefully, and we trust them," says Ray Lewis. "They're on the honor system."

So was Dennis Levine.

Stock watching is only one facet of proxy solicitors' M&A services—and only one avenue through which they gain inside information. In virtually all takeovers, a pair of proxy firms are enlisted. Working alongside the lawyers, these agents of corporate warfare vie for the shareholders' votes that are critical to the objectives of each side.

Enlisted at the earliest stages of a takeover—or to identify, through their stock-watch services, assaults in the making— proxy firms operate like the infamous precinct captains who have long dominated Chicago politics. Their job is to get out the vote and to get it out in favor of the side employing their services— the raider or management—however that has to be done. In the process,. they court and intimidate the shareholders, sweet-talk the institutions, woo the arbs, write love letters, write hate letters, threaten their adversaries and finally count the votes. Always count the votes.

As key players on the M&A team, the proxy firms are another of the schools of insiders that swim through the takeover business, absorbing confidential information on hundreds of secret deals. Here, as with the attorneys, the commercial and investment bankers, the consultants and the management confidants, the opportunities for proxy solicitors to obtain corporate intelligence and use it for personal gain are enormous. They represent another gaping hole in the veneer of secrecy said to protect against market manipulation.

Compounding matters is the fact that proxy solicitation is a dirty business dominated by three firms that spend much of their time slinging mud at each other. The newest of the breed—The Carter Organization—also happens to be the most aggressive of the bunch. Run by gravel-voiced, motor-mouthed Don Carter, the fifteen-year-old firm has stolen the thunder from its relatively ancient competitors, D. F. King (established 1942) and Georgeson & Company (founded 1936.)

Carter, who worked previously as an analyst for takeover ace turned reluctant airline president Carl Icahn, has rewritten the rules for proxy solicitation, changing it from a rather methodical vote-courting and -tabulating service to an active consultancy that creates and implements takeover strategies for a bevy of corporate raiders. The Carter Organization's thirty-eight-year-old president, whose prematurely gray hair and bloodshot eyes make him look a decade older, couldn't be cockier about it.

"When I started this business, I didn't know shit from Shinola about proxy solicitations," says Carter, who's known on the Street as a piece of work, a wild man and the world's greatest fan of Don Carter. "All I knew was that the established firms were resting on their laurels, certain that they could monopolize the business as they'd done for years. Because they weren't serving clients—weren't giving them what they wanted or needed—I knew there was an opportunity for a kid from Brooklyn who could fill that void."

He glances at his wristwatch. "It's nine-ten A.M. now, right? Take any top executive at King—say, Art Long, John Gavin or any of the others—and I guarantee you that if we call them now they won't be in the office yet. . . . They're in a business that lives and breathes by the stock exchanges and they come in after the markets open."

"Not here. I come in at seven-thirty," continues Carter, "and my clients know if that's not early enough, they can reach me at home twenty-four hours a day. How? They have my home phone number. I gave that out the day I went into business."

"King's a joke. They have a reputation for being a brawling, hard-driving group that gets the job done. But if you want to find them . . . just drop in at Michael's Two [a Wall Street area restaurant]. That's where they are.

"King's top guy, Art Long, doesn't even remember peoples' names. He calls everyone 'kid' or 'rascal.' Well, you don't get away with that with Saul Steinberg [a Carter client]. You don't refer to Saul as 'kid.'"

The King–Georgeson crowd are no less bashful about airing their opinions of the "kid from Brooklyn." In what is truly a cultural as well as professional clash—Carter sees it as the Long Island Jew against the downtown WASPs—both sides try to hit where it hurts. For the King–Georgeson camp that means pointing to the record, a record they insist shows Carter to be little more than PR hype.

"Carter never—well, make that hardly ever—wins," snarls Georgeson president (and son of the firm's cofounder) Richard Nye. Polished, patrician and born to his position, he is everything Carter is not. "Don's strategy on proxy battles is to come barging into a contest, talk tough, make a lot of noise and get a lot of press coverage for himself.

"It's a diversionary tactic. If he's quoted as saying tough things, if he mouths off about winning, people won't notice how poor his record really is. They'll fall for the façade, for the tough-guy image, and hire him anyway. That's Carter's strategy."

To support his claim, Nye unveils a scorecard of major proxy contests (waged from December 1983 to June 1986), showing Georgeson with twenty-one victories and Carter with a lowly four.

GEORGESON & CO. INC.
PROXY CONTESTS
GULF OIL TO PRESENT

Date	Winner	Solicitor	Loser	Solicitor
12/02/83	Gulf Oil	Georgeson and King	Pickens	Carter
1/30/84	NJR	Georgeson	N.U.I.	Carter
3/14/84	Asher Edelman	Hill & Knowlton	M.A.I.	Georgeson and Carter
4/06/84	I.R.E. Financial	Georgeson	Atlantic Federal	Carter
6/12/84	G. C. Murphy	Georgeson	Arveron	Carter
6/14/84	Tweedy Browne	Georgeson	1st Federal Roanoke	Schroder
6/21/84	Rooney Pace	Carter	Norlin	Georgeson and King
7/26/84	Carter Hawley Hale	Georgeson and King	The Limited	Carter
9/11/84	Woodward & Lothrop	Georgeson	Shareholders' Committee	Carter
10/24/84	Shareholders' Committee	Georgeson	Florida Federal	Kissel-Blake
12/06/84	Pantry Pride	Carter	Shareholders' Committee	Georgeson and King
12/12/84	City Investing	Georgeson	Tamco	Carter

165

Date	Winner	Solicitor	Loser	Solicitor
1/28/85	Shareholders' Committee	Georgeson	Fortune Financial	Carter
2/08/85	Woodhead Ind.	King	Nortek	Georgeson
4/26/85	Peter Bermont	Georgeson	Heritage Federal	Morrow
5/06/85	Hilton Hotels	Georgeson	Golden Nugget	Carter
5/09/85	Informatics General	Georgeson	Sterling Software	Carter
5/14/85	Gulf Resources	Georgeson and Morrow	Shareholders' Committee	Carter
6/11/85	Sun Equities	Carter	Patrick Industries	Georgeson
6/18/85	Shareholders' Committee	Georgeson	Vega Biotechnologies	None
1/21/86	Atlantic Federal S&L	Georgeson	M. Lee Pearce	None
1/24/86	Woodhead Ind.	King	Nortek	Georgeson
2/11/86	British Commonwealth Shipping	Georgeson	Telerate	King
2/18/86	Clevetrust Realty Investors	Carter	Robert Goodman	Georgeson
2/28/86	Baird Corp.	Georgeson	Shareholders' Committee	Carter
5/01/86	Fruehauf Corp.	Georgeson	Asher Edelman	Hill & Knowlton
5/06/86	Shareholders' Committee	Georgeson	Regal International	Carter
5/14/86	First Federal S&L of Kalamazoo	Hill & Knowlton	Shareholders' Committee	Georgeson
5/17/86	CTS	Georgeson	Dynamicas Corp. of America	Carter

Georgeson's Record: W–21, L–8
Georgeson 14 vs. Carter 4

While the record appears to support Georgeson's claim of superiority, a nagging question remains. If Carter is incompetent, ineffective and so clearly inferior to his venerable competitors, why is he hired by the smartest whips in American business, the men who hate to lose—at anything? Why do the Steinbergs, the Pickenses and the Icahns count themselves as loyal Carter clients when they could easily walk across the street to the competition?

Carter, who stages an Oscar-winning fit the first time he scans the Georgeson scorecard, deftly folds the evidence into a paper airplane and glides it across the room.

"This . . . this fish wrapping says that our client, Boone Pickens, lost the Gulf deal," Carter says, forcing out a mechanical chuckle. "Do you know Boone and his group walked away from that deal with $750 million in profit? If that's the definition of losing, Christ, no wonder I have so many clients."

To Carter, who claims to play a more intimate role in shaping his client's strategies than do King or Georgeson, only those with a Paleolithic view of the proxy process would rate solicitors on a won/lost basis. Amassing votes is not the acid test, he insists. Making money for the client, whether he wins the vote or not, is the bottom line.

How Carter came to work with T. Boone Pickens and how he helped mastermind the assault of Gulf illustrates how proxy solicitors are absorbed into the circle of insiders and how they gain access to a wealth of confidential information.

Carter first joined the Pickens camp in the fall of 1983. At the time, the Texas takeover king and his Gulf Investors Group (Mike Boswell of Sunshine Mining; brothers Sam, Hy and Bill of the Canadian Belzberg family; Cyril Wagner, Jr., and Jack Brown of the oil and gas outfit Wagner & Brown; and John Habbert III of Habbert International, a Southern real estate venture) were sitting in the bulrushes with some 11 percent of Gulf stock, planning an all-out blitzkrieg on the sluggish oil giant. Gulf management learned of the group's secret accumulations through its own Wall Street sources and called a special meeting of the stockholders for December 2.

"The sole purpose of the meeting," Carter says, "was to impede a Pickens takeover by changing Gulf's incorporation from Pennsylvania to Delaware. How would that defend against

Boone? Because at that point Gulf's bylaws allowed for so-called 'cumulative voting.' Put simply, this granted to stockholders the right to cast—for every share of stock they owned—thirteen votes in elections to the board of directors. They could cast one vote for each of the board's thirteen seats or—and this is what unnerved Gulf's management—could stack all thirteen for any single nominee. With this all-in-one provision [cumulative voting] a shareholder with only slightly more than seven percent of Gulf stock could assure himself a seat on the board."

Viewing this prospect as the corporate equivalent of a plunge into a pool of barracudas, Gulf's management sought the protection of Delaware law, which prohibits cumulative voting.

Learning of Gulf's intentions, on October 23, 1983, Pickens gathered his fellow raiders for an emergency skull-session at the offices of the prominent Houston law firm Baker & Botts. Also attending this top-secret powwow was an M&A specialist from Lehman Brothers, then serving as the group's investment banker, and Don Carter, whose firm Pickens had selected as his proxy solicitor only days before.

As this colorful menagerie of Canadian sharks, Wall Street operatives and Sunbelt wheeler-dealers went into the meeting, it was assumed—on the basis of previous telephone conversations—that they would fight the antitakeover measure by countering with a proposal on royalty trusts. This would require Gulf to distribute all of the income from its oil wells directly to shareholders, rather than allow management to allocate the money for other investments, which at Gulf had turned out to be disastrous over the years.

But Carter argued for a more direct approach. A proxy fight pitting the royalty trust against cumulative voting would, he argued, only confuse the shareholders because both are arcane and complicated issues. Instead, he counseled for an all-out goal-line defense against reincorporation.

In the end, the group agreed with Carter and proceeded with a singleminded proxy fight to stop Gulf from reincorporating in Delaware—a fight they would quickly lose. Although the raiders made a strong case against management's plan, when the results were tallied, Gulf (which was represented by a team of proxy solicitors from Georgeson and King) held 52.7 percent of the outstanding shares—enough to proceed with the reincorporation.

But it was far from a decisive victory. Considering that it held the advantage of incumbency, the margin of victory had to be a disappointment to Gulf and for the same reason a sign of encouragement to the investor group. With that in mind, Carter unleashed the tactics that have made him the solicitor of choice for Wall Street's most ruthless carnivores:

"We knew Gulf was vulnerable. So after the stockholder meeting was concluded—after Gulf walked away the apparent victor in that first proxy contest—we tightened the screws, letting them know, in no uncertain terms, that we weren't giving up or going away. As part of our offensive, we took out full-page newspaper ads stating that we would not give up, would not go away and, in fact, would continue to accumulate Gulf shares."

On January 5, 1984, a defeated but undaunted Pickens called for another brainstorming session at Baker & Botts. Attending were the members of the Gulf Investors Group, the lawyers, the Lehman Brothers banker and Don Carter, who took center stage to explain to this clan how the Gulf voting had broken down and what could now be done to gain control of the company.

Carter's message was bold and optimistic. In carefully examining the proxies, he made a critical discovery: of the shareholders in Gulf's 52.7 percent majority, 15 percent had already sold their stock. Most of these pivotal shares had since moved from mom and pop stockholders, including current and retired Gulf employees, to the arbitragers who were playing Gulf as a takeover stock. Unlike the mom and pop shareholders who were inclined to stick with Gulf's management, the arbs would be loyal to the highest bidder; the Pickens group could thus count on their proxies in future elections.

"A lot of the stock was now held by institutions, arbs and hot money brokers," Carter says, "all of whom had made money betting on Pickens in the past and were likely to go with him again."

On the basis of this analysis, Carter, who was clearly stepping out of his role as vote counter and into that of takeover guru, advised the group—which now held 13 percent of Gulf's shares—to tender for an additional 12 percent, bringing their holdings to 25 percent. This, coupled with the stock of share-holding arbs he believed would vote with the Pickens group on the next go-round, would be enough to gain control of the company.

But just as Carter put the finishing touches on his battle plan, Sam Belzberg reportedly interrupted with an even bolder strategy of his own: a preemptive strike against Gulf Oil.

"Sam said, 'Why go for twelve percent of the stock when we can go for fifty-one percent and be sure of gaining control?'" Carter recalls. "I'd never suggested this because of the huge capital requirement—about four billion—that would be required above and beyond what the group had already committed in acquiring their thirteen-percent stake. But that didn't seem to faze the investors, so we spent the next hour or so discussing the fifty-one-percent idea."

It was then that one of the investors suggested to Pickens, in a whisper so that the Lehman man in the room could not hear, that they switch investment bankers, replacing Lehman (which at the time was considered out of its league in a $4 billion financing) with Drexel Burnham, whose West Coast–based junk-bond operation could deliver the money to fund the Gulf takeover. A man with an antenna for dollars, Pickens liked the idea from the start and flew immediately to Drexel Burnham's Beverly Hills command post to outline his plan.

"At first, Drexel came up with an intricate scheme to raise the war chest and acquire the fifty-one percent of Gulf stock," Carter remembers. "But that plan was later dropped in favor of a quick-strike tender offer for eight percent of Gulf's shares. Added to what the investors already controlled [thirteen percent] and to the sympathetic shares sitting with the arbs, Drexel believed that eight percent would be sufficient to gain control of the company. What's more, going for eight rather than fifty-one percent meant the group could act with lightning speed and that was important. Because the goal was to keep the pressure on Gulf, time was of the essence.

"The strategy worked like a Swiss watch. The eight-percent tender offer—which we never even got to complete—spelled the end of Gulf Oil. As soon as we filed for it, Gulf feared our gaining control of the company so much that they went to Socal, which had positioned itself as a white knight. Proof positive that they weren't willing to risk a proxy fight on their own."

Pickens's original plan, to gain control of the company, had failed. But when Socal bought out the stockholders, the Gulf Investors Group took gains of $750 million, with Pickens's Mesa Petroleum claiming more than half, about $400 million.

"Georgeson's silly little scorecard would have you believe that the Carter organization—and in turn Boone Pickens and friends—lost the December 2 proxy battle," Carter says. "But only a firm whose vision is limited to counting proxies could say that. We don't suffer from that myopia. We count dollars. Our goal is to make money for our clients—lots of money—whether we win the votes or not."

Not surprisingly, his competitors at D. F. King hold markedly different views of the proxy business in general and of the battle for Gulf Oil. But in spite of their differences, they are remarkably alike in their status as insiders.

When we meet King president and co-owner Arthur Long, he is settling into his throne for a long, rambling lunch at his favorite hangout, Michael's Two. Long leans back into a high Naugahyde club chair and launches into an overview of the proxy and M&A business. A big, proud, back-slapping man—who played football at Columbia University and who in the 1960s represented some of the early conglomerators, including Gulf & Western's Charley Bluhdorn and Ling-Temco-Vought's Jimmy Ling—Long has a knack common to elder statesmen. He can cite the ingredients for success in his business.

"You want to know how to succeed in proxy solicitation? I can explain it to you in a nutshell. [Proxy lawyer George] Demas, God bless his soul, taught me this lesson. . . . You're writing letters to the stockholders and soon enough you learn that they care about one thing and one thing alone. That they bought the stock for thirty dollars and now it's down to twenty. They're mad. How do you, as management, get that guy's vote when he's not at all happy with the way the stock's performed under your leadership? I'll tell you. By getting him madder at the other guy than he is at you. By telling him the other guy's stock has done worse than yours. That the other guy can't manage. That the other guy's been indicted. Whatever.

"You see, the biggest single issue in a proxy fight is doubt. The side that can create doubt is the winner. If you're representing management in a hostile takeover, you want to create doubt among the shareholders. Doubt that the raider can raise the financing. Doubt that he can hold the financing together. Doubt that he's paying a fair price for the company. Once you've created doubt, it's more likely the shareholders will stay with you."

Long, a confidant to takeover artists when Carter was still in school, continues: "The last time I saw Carter I said, 'Hey, rascal, when you going to win one already?' Of the last five big battles, he'd posted a perfect score—zero for five. . . . He now throws around this nonsense that losing isn't losing if the client makes money. The truth is he lost on Gulf. When you hold Boone's stock out of the results, the free shares voted three to one for us. And as to the nonsense that we don't get involved in strategy planning, hell, I was in it from the start.

"In early September 1983, I was summoned by Gulf's executive vice-president Harold Hammer, who hired us to represent the company. Soon after coming on board, we found that Boone was accumulating Gulf shares. By the time he filed his 13-D [the SEC document that must be filed when an investor acquires 5 percent or more of a company's stock] in October, we knew precisely what was happening. We attended about a dozen strategy meetings with the Gulf team, which included ourselves, Sullivan and Cromwell, Salomon Brothers and Kekst, deciding eventually to go for a reincorporation that would allow us to eliminate the cumulative voting.

"It was a smart move. If we didn't do that, we believed Boone would continue to buy enough Gulf stock to assure his people two seats on the board by the time of the annual meeting in April. So the decision was to fight him from a position of strength in December rather than fight him from weakness in the spring. And we won at that, getting the reincorporation and knocking out the cumulative voting."

Of Carter's claim that Gulf caved in when Pickens went for more of its stock, "Bullshit," Long retorts. "The board simply decided, in the interest of the Gulf shareholders, to take the best offer it could get for the company. And let's face it, if you want to talk about bottom line, the sum ultimately offered by Socal was about the highest ever paid for oil reserves.

"I can't run the company," Long says, referring to Gulf—and, indirectly, to the other clients King represents. "The board of directors does that. Our job is to win the proxy contest—and we did."

Regardless of who won or lost the proxy battle or indeed the war in the Gulf–Pickens struggle, it is clear that the proxy solicitors for both sides are early insiders, privy to advance information that could make them wealthy or wealthier, as the case may be, were they to trade on it. But do they use this access for personal profit? Do they trade on the knowledge that clients will be Pac-Manning other publicly held companies?

"Never," Carter says. "This firm prohibits anyone, including myself, from trading in any stocks we learn about through what could be classified as inside information. All securities purchases, whether we think they have anything to do with inside information or not, have to be cleared through our house counsel, Dennis Mensch, and as a further precaution, employees are required to sign an agreement that the confidential information they gain through their work here will be kept confidential. We ban leaks and we ban inside trading."

But some say that the boss's personal investments make for a conflict of interest. Consider Carter's status as a limited partner in the arbitrage house of S. B. Lewis. According to his critics, this constitutes playing both sides of the street. In his roles as proxy solicitor and confidant to corporate raiders, Carter is in position to gain valuable, nonpublic information, information he may be tempted to pass on to the Lewis firm, profiting as a partner in the take should they trade in the stocks he touts.

A charge Carter denies: "So what about Lewis? I've never used that association for anything illegal or unethical. First of all, Sandy Lewis is as straight as an arrow. If I called him with information, he'd slam the phone down on me. And there's no real motive for me to tell them anything anyway. My interest is only a half-million-dollar investment in a billion-dollar outfit. The gain, were there any, wouldn't filter down to me."

There is no reason to doubt him. But Carter's personal investments are indicative of the complex interrelationships between the coterie of Wall Street players who seem to pop up around the endless series of mergers, acquisitions and leveraged buyouts that have reshaped American business.

Asked if a proxy solicitor's position as a limited partner in an arb house is a conflict of interest, SEC enforcement chief Gary Lynch (the man who collared Dennis Levine) says, "I wouldn't use those words."

What words would he use?

"It creates a situation where there may be temptations. But there are thousands of those temptations on Wall Street every day. The important point is whether people succumb to them or not."

Like Carter, both Long and his executive vice-president John Gavin (who sources say runs the firm and is responsible for planning most of its proxy battles) insist that they never trade on inside information, although Long admits that word of the firm's activities could leak down the chain of command even to secretaries and receptionists: "Who the hell would know if they're telling their boyfriends to buy a stock?" Carter too admits that he cannot police his staff. The greatest safeguard, he says, is in "knowing the kind of people you hire, the kind of people you allow access to the information." But is that a reliable safeguard? Didn't employers at Lehman Brothers and Drexel Burnham think that they "knew" Dennis Levine?

The truth is that an employer's primary concern, especially in the results-oriented environment of M&A, is whether the employee can do the job. According to Wall Street's unofficial credo that good guys finish last, high moral fiber may be seen as more of a minus than a plus. The takeover sharks have long prided themselves on being irreverent iconoclasts making their fortunes outfoxing the corporate establishment. The hired hands they favor at the law firms, proxy houses, PR mills and investment banks are the street fighters, angle players, schemers and calculators who create the best deals and make them work. These same people are often masters of deception.

"Look," says Long, "there's always been insider trading. It's pervasive—more widespread than people want to admit. From what I've learned, the SEC's coming down on thirty-five more. Thirty-five more fools who thought they could be pigs and get away with it. When I stop to think about it, one thought goes around in my head: some people are very, very stupid."

Others would come to say the same thing about a promising Lehman Brothers vice-president, Dennis Levine, who was about to open up a grand new phase in his financial master plan as a recruit of the premier M&A investment firm, Drexel Burnham Lambert.

IX

Wheeling and Dealing in Drexel Land

"You know the yuppie national anthem. It's the Michelob Light commercial that goes, 'Who says you can't have it all?' Well, by the end of 1984, Dennis seemed to be the guy they wrote the lyrics about. He was rising at Lehman, he had a lovely son, Adam, and a knock-out wife and he was still shy of thirty-five years old. You had to envy the guy. That's without even knowing that he already had millions stashed away in a Bahamian bank account."
—A former friend and colleague of Dennis Levine, who now wants to see him "fry" for what he's done to investment banking

By the time Shearson American Express—the fast-growing financial services outfit—purchased Lehman Brothers in the spring of 1984, Dennis Levine was a modestly wealthy man. With about $3.5 million in his Bank Leu account and a six-figure vice-president's salary coming in from Lehman, he had achieved a level of affluence his parents and their Bayside neighbors could only dream about. But it wasn't enough.

"Lehman's sale to Shearson brought mixed blessings for Levine," says a former Lehman vice-president. "Although he was doing good work at the firm, he wasn't universally liked. There were two camps there. One, the white-shoes, viewed investment banking as a gentlemanly profession, through which you rose on the basis of old school ties. Because Dennis didn't conform to their definition of *gentlemen*—his being Jewish didn't help—and because he didn't have old school ties—did you ever hear of anyone having lunch at the Baruch Club?—they considered Levine and his kind a pox on the firm. Were it up to them, Dennis would go nowhere—except maybe to a used-car lot where they thought he belonged.

"The other major faction, what I call the Jewish Defense League, was made up of young, aggressive, mostly Jewish guys who wore spikes instead of white shoes. The only rules they played by were the ones that got the deals done. This group, which came into power after the merger, felt just the opposite about Dennis. They considered him a valuable asset to the firm. Dennis basked in it for a while."

But only for a while. Tempting as it may have been for Levine to stay on at Lehman, where he was secretly getting rich on a steady flow of inside information, the downside of the Shearson merger prompted him to write a new resumé. With Lehman having relinquished its 134-year status as a privately held firm, all the young ladder-climbers who had joined the firm with the ultimate goal of "making partner" found their fondest ambition cut from under them like an expired option. No matter how they distinguished themselves, they could never own a piece of the equity. Lehman Brothers was now a subsidiary of a publicly held company. The stockholders were the owners. Everyone else, including the investment bankers, was an employee.

To Levine this was unacceptable. Like dozens of others who caused the firm to suffer through a near mutiny as some of the most talented M&A people departed for more promising environs, he found the new setup repugnant and sought to land a partnership position in one of the few big firms still private at the time.

His chances were excellent. The M&A market seemed immune to the cyclical decline some observers had predicted and was going through its most explosive phase. The major investment banks were chronically short of senior talent, making a bright VP with deal-making experience at what had been one of the busiest firms on the Street about as hard a sell as a thousand-yard gainer in the NFL draft.

"Dennis knew that he was highly marketable and he used that knowledge to manipulate his negotiations in the job market," says a former Lehman colleague. "When most guys look for jobs, they go CIA. Hush-hush, top-secret, no-one-knows-but-their-wives kind of thing.

"But Dennis had a better idea. Just as the White House leaks news to manipulate public opinion, he'd do the same at Lehman. By letting his superiors get wind of the fact that he was talking with others, he knew they'd be inclined to put a little padding in his paycheck. Not that that would be enough to keep him. He had more on his mind than a raise. But getting Lehman to up the ante would force his subsequent employer to pay all that much more to snare him. In effect, he was just raising the minimum bid before auctioning off his services.

"Dennis always knew how to market himself. While climbing the ladder at Lehman, he made sure that all the heavies knew what he was up to and how well he was performing on a given deal. In this way, when the fee was paid everyone thought he'd contributed, whether he did or not. Actually that was part of the Lehman culture—for every ten guys who worked on a deal, twenty took credit for it. Dennis just turned it into an art form. He was an expert at self-promotion."

Levine's career ambition was fulfilled when Drexel hired the Wall Street headhunting firm of Hadley Lockwood to find a senior-level banker for its burgeoning M&A department. Having tracked his career—identifying him as a rising young star—Hadley executive Dave Hart thought Dennis ideal for the job and called him in for a meeting. Levine, who usually wore a poker face to these sessions, learned early in the interview that Hart was recruiting for Drexel and acted like a child who has just seen the tooth fairy. Having harbored an ambition to work for the hottest investment bank on the Street—a description even Drexel's competitors admitted it deserved—Levine found the opportunity staring him in the face. Starting at Drexel on February 1, 1985, he was guaranteed $1 million in his rookie year as an M&A managing director.

It was a match made in heaven. Hot, aggressive, iconoclastic, Drexel was shaking up investment banking with its hardball tactics and its creative approach to mergers and acquisitions. Just coming into its own as an M&A powerhouse, Drexel needed hungry and freewheeling dealmakers to tap its bubbling potential. With the firm's West Coast wunderkind Mike Milken creating a striking new mechanism for financing mergers through the issuance of low-rated debt instruments known as junk bonds, Drexel needed rainmakers to ferret out prospective deals that would fly with the aid of Milken's junk-bond financing.

Levine was perfect for the role. Unlike Lehman Brothers and

the other ancient firms that prided themselves on collegiality and tradition, Drexel focused singlemindedly on results. To the white-shoes at Lehman, who disliked and mistrusted Levine, the order of priorities was gentleman first, investment banker second. The view at Drexel was that gentlemen belong at law firms or at Harvard, not in investment banking. The players at laissez-faire Drexel likened the white-shoes to the Dan Aykroyd character in the movie *Ghostbusters*. When told that his job as a professor is in jeopardy, he responds, "I can't go to the private sector. They expect results there."

"For Dennis, the decision to leave Lehman and come here was a layup," says a Drexel executive who worked with Levine within days of his arrival. "First, he'd come from a firm where they'd done a million deals to one where volume was first perking up, so he'd be one of the real experienced people. He'd stand out from the crowd. Second, he'd go from being the second or third guy on a deal to the guy in charge. Third, they'd double his salary. Fourth, they'd make him a managing director. Fifth, and perhaps most important, Dennis knew that no one here—at least none of the senior guys—would think he was too aggressive or too ambitious or too brash. That's exactly the kind of guys we wanted.

"Why? Because we haven't gone to bed with the corporate establishment—with the Roger Smiths of GM or the Ackers of IBM. Instead our clients are the Saul Steinbergs and Carl Icahns who've given shock treatments to the corporate guys and who expect their bankers to save the white gloves for weddings. To these guys, good investment bankers are like good entrepreneurs: fast and loose and hungry. If they didn't have a Dennis Levine, they'd have to create one."

Sitting across the bargaining table from Levine, Mike Zimmerman, Salomon Brothers' M&A chieftain, saw evidence of this. "In the few times I met Dennis, I thought he was too fast; irresponsible. In one situation, I represented the owner of a privately held business. Sam Belzberg, whom Dennis represented, wanted to buy my client's company. But my man was leery of dealing with Belzberg because of his reputation as a shark. Instead of dissuading my client of this fear, instead of proving himself to be reasonable, Belzberg warned my guy that he had until five that afternoon to make his decision or else the deal would be off. You couldn't come up with a worse approach if you wanted to.

"Dennis, for his part, did nothing to smooth out the deal. He appeared to encourage Belzberg throughout and Belzberg seemed to love him for it."

Adds Steven Key, a senior partner with the accounting firm of Arthur Young; "Levine was not quantitatively oriented. There are guys over at Morgan Stanley who run rings around him technically. But he was very aggressive. He pushed things right to the line. He always wanted to know how far he could stretch a transaction before it broke."

It was clear that at Drexel Levine would find more than a home. He would find a culture he could thrive in. But a question remains: why did he care? With his Bank Leu account ballooning like a hot computer stock, with his insider trading scheme proving virtually foolproof, why be tempted by Drexel's generous checkbook and the perks of partnership? Why be concerned about a career at all when extracurricular activities were bound to make him one of the richest men on Wall Street? If he were to rise to the chairmanship of Drexel, his legitimate earnings would pale in comparison to his Bank Leu account and to the secret commission deal he'd worked out with Ivan Boesky.

To some observers of the Levine odyssey, the Lehman-to-Drexel move had more to do with access than equity.

"Dennis wanted to move to Drexel for one reason and one reason alone," says a Prudential-Bache senior executive. "As a partner, he'd be wired into developing deals at an earlier stage. Translation: better and faster information.

"In the deal business, every transaction starts off with a tiny core of insiders, perhaps the acquirer and his closest business associates. They identify the target they want to pursue, do a little homework on it, and then call in an investment banker and maybe a senior law-firm partner.

"In this foreplay period, knowledge of the prospective takeover is limited to the high-level contacts in the law firms and investment banks who get the first call. Gradually, as the deal unfolds, but is not yet made public, a wider array of insiders—including more lawyers, investment bankers, proxy people and accountants—are brought in to work on it. At Smith Barney and at Lehman, Dennis got this second-wave information. But by becoming a Drexel managing director—and thus running the deals himself—he knew he'd be among the first to get inside information, and that was what he was after. That's why he left Lehman."

Another Dennis-watcher, a partner in a takeover law firm, sees it differently: "Levine walked from Lehman because the merger threatened to siphon the entrepreneurial juices out of that firm—meaning it wouldn't be a fun place to work anymore—and because for the first time in his life people would be bidding for his services. He knew full well that at that period in the mergers-and-acquisitions market, that he'd be as hot as a Hula Hoop in the fifties. To have Wall Street's most prominent firms bidding against each other for your services—that had to feel pretty damned terrific to a thirty-something-year-old who only a few years before had to sweep the floors to get a job down here."

Whether Levine left Lehman for access or ego or partnership may never be known, but one thing seems clear: his greed knew no bounds. Like the square-jawed, suspender-sporting, steely-eyed yuppies in the Michelob Light commercials, he believed he could have it all. To Levine that meant a legitimate career and an illegal trading scheme that encompassed a ring of Wall Street spies, cash payoffs, code names, Bahamian rendezvous and Swiss bank accounts. So driven was he to achieve the new Wall Street dream of being rich before age thirty-five (to Levine *rich* meant $100 million) that he was determined to pursue every avenue to make it a reality. Yes, his Drexel salary would pale when compared to his market gains and his Boesky payoffs, but they would still add millions to the cache and would provide a convenient cover for the high life-style he was determined to live.

Levine's arrival at Drexel in February 1985 was greeted with the same mix of joy and jealousy as when a hot new running back enters an NFL summer camp. To the coach and the quarterback he's the offensive messiah they've each been clasping their hands for. To the reigning star of the backfield, it's "let's prove the new guy stinks" time. Convincing both factions that you're a worthy contender takes a minor miracle. Dennis pulled it off like Herschel Walker scoring from the two.

"Most of the partners welcomed Dennis as this hotshot Lehman guy, who, legend had it, was capable of great things," says an attorney who has represented Drexel in dozens of deals. "If he was as good as his supporters claimed, he'd bring more money to the firm, enriching them all. Nothing to argue about.

"But those lower down in the Drexel pecking order—mostly the first VPs Dennis had leapfrogged in his route to partnership—saw his coming as a threat. Why, they complained, should this thirty-three-year-old be plucked from the VP ranks at Lehman to be transformed, like Cinderella, into a Drexel partner? The very promotion they'd been toiling in house for.

"As you can imagine, this group prayed that Dennis would fall on his face, crumble under the pressure, prove himself unworthy of partnership. Anything to get him out of there and to open that slot for the Drexies who thought it was rightfully theirs. But that wasn't in the cards. Dennis was good—damn good. Something they learned very, very fast."

Thrown into major deals at the outset, Levine found somewhat to his dismay that Drexel's talent at the M&A partner level was often weak and disoriented, markedly inferior to the more experienced Lehmanites at whose side he had learned to do deals. With Drexel first emerging as an M&A force, partners and VPs alike were rushed into deal-making positions without the personal assets or the practical experience to pull them off. Clearly in over their heads, they sometimes came up with really harebrained schemes.

Case in point: With his sights set on a possible takeover of Phillips Petroleum, Drexel client Carl Icahn approached the firm's M&A department for the money to tender for Phillips stock. While Drexel could easily raise the cash through Mike Milken's junk-bond network, Icahn would be saddled with $7.5 million in commitment fees payable to the investor group. To shift that liability from Icahn to a third party, one of Drexel's reigning M&A "geniuses" had the bright idea of dumping the fees on the arbs, many of whom were sitting with stockpiles of Phillips stock and would profit handsomely from an Icahn take-over.

But as attractive as the fee-shifting plan might be to Icahn, Levine knew instinctively that it was stupid and, more important, not doable.

"There'd be all sorts of complications," says a former Drexel associate, "including an expansion of the investor group—which you'd want to avoid—and a brush with the securities laws, which probably would rule against it. But if by some miracle you could find some way to get around all of that, you'd still have to convince the arbs to pony up the money; and my God, anyone with experience in the real world knows that crowd doesn't pony up money so fast. Not to take a load off another investor. Bottom line: it was one fuckin' dumb idea.

"But Dennis was too much of a political animal to tell the guy who dreamed up the plan, 'Hey man, this is the stupidest thing in the world.' Instead, he pulled the guy aside and said, 'I hear what you want to do, but if you do that then you'll have to consider that these three things will happen.' Dennis goes on to list the legal problems and the arb problems and so on, and suddenly the . . . former genius who dreamed up the fee-switching scheme realizes it's something that can't be done and scotches the plan.

"That was Dennis's great skill. Getting another partner to change his plan without getting that partner—who'd been at Drexel much longer than Dennis—pissed off at him. A valuable talent in a political hotbed like Drexel Burnham. Anyone can give advice. Knowing how to give it—that's what set Dennis apart.

"He worked the same magic with clients, proving himself a valuable addition to the firm from day one. How'd he do it? Let's say he knew where a client stood on a deal, and he also knew where he had to get that client to make the deal fly. His job was to shift that client from position X to position Z. How? By pushing the client? By forcing the issue? No, that wasn't Dennis's style. Instead [as he did with the partner in the Icahn financing], he'd give the client just enough information so that the client himself would see the wisdom of going from X to Z.

"What if the client was obstinate, flatly refusing to go to Z? No problem. That's when Dennis the Diplomat would emerge, saying 'Okay, let's not go to Z. But how about going to Y, a place between X and Z?' His approach: get the client to the midpoint today; tomorrow nudge him over to Z.

"Dennis knew when to back off, when to push, when to be subtle and when to be merciless."

Soon after arriving at Drexel, Levine—perhaps taken with his newly elevated status as "investment banking managing director"—began to live the part, moving from his plain vanilla Fifty-seventh Street rental apartment to a showplace co-op at 1185 Park Avenue.

"For Dennis, moving to Park Avenue was like Sir Edmund Hillary planting his flag on Mount Everest," says a friend of Levine's wife, Laurie. "He always equated Park Avenue with old money, with serious money, with his heroes on Wall Street. In fact, as stately a building as 1185 is, to Dennis it was just a way station. His ultimate goal was to buy a place at 740 Park, where Saul Steinberg lives. He needed millions for that—and he was working on it."

Was he ever. If partnership led him to Park Avenue, it also inflated his trading goals, prompting Dennis to take huge positions and, in turn, to score enormous gains on takeover-related issues. His biggest score to that point came in January 1985, when The Coastal Corporation retained Drexel Burnham in connection with a possible tender offer for the stock of American National Resources (ANR). Involved as he was in lining up the financing for Coastal's still secret bid, Levine was privy to the company's strategy and was aware that a takeover bid was imminent.

In testimony to the SEC, John Sorte, a Drexel managing director and head of its energy group, recalled the events leading up to the Coastal deal.

"[From] January 14 to 16, 1985, I attended a series of meetings in New York and Los Angeles with representatives from Coastal to discuss the possibility of seeking financing for a combination with ANR. This was the first time that the identity of ANR was disclosed to me. In order to keep confidential ANR's identity in this transaction, the company was initially given the code name GULL.

"During the next ten days I met on and off with representatives from Coastal concerning various financing possibilities for their proposed acquisition of ANR. On or about January 25, 1985, I was advised by Coastal that the deal as originally contemplated had been called off.

"Beginning in late January 1985, I turned my attention to another transaction involving our client The Icahn Group and its interest in Phillips Petroleum. Assisting me on this transaction was Dennis B. Levine, who had just joined Drexel on February 1, 1985, as managing director in our mergers-and-acquisitions group. Mr. Levine was assigned to work with me on this transaction both as an observer so that he could see firsthand how a transaction such as this was handled at Drexel, and also to provide me with strategic input from a merger-and-acquisition perspective.

"On the evening of February 11 or 12, 1985, I received a telephone call from David Arledge, Coastal's senior vice-president. At that time, Mr. Levine and I were working on the Icahn–Phillips transaction at the law offices of Gordon Hurwitz Butowsky Weitzen Shalov & Wein. Mr. Arledge advised me that, since we last met at the end of January, Coastal had been exploring alternative sources of financing for its acquisition of ANR and now wanted to again discuss using the services of Drexel.

"During our telephone conversation, Mr. Arledge related to me that the anticipated terms of the deal were as we had previously discussed in January, including the part that it was to be an all-cash offer and the contemplated dollar amount. I shortly thereafter relayed the information provided to me by Mr. Arledge to Mr. Levine, who was present at the law offices when the call came in. The information provided to me by Mr. Arledge and furnished to Mr. Levine was confidential.

"After receiving the above-described telephone call from Mr. Arledge, I relayed to Mr. Levine my enthusiasm about the Coastal–ANR transaction. First, it was an all-cash transaction using high-yield debt securities. The fact that it was all cash in my view increased its chance of success. Second, the transaction involved a pipeline acquiring another pipeline in a context that made good business sense. Finally, the range of per-share prices being discussed for the tender offer was, in my view, a top-dollar price.

"Over the weekend of February 15 to 17, 1985, Coastal executives flew to New York to meet with Drexel representatives including Mr. Levine and myself, as well as representatives of certain banks to outline possible transaction and financing terms. We continued to work through the week and on February 24, 1985, the engagement letter was amended in a letter executed by Dennis Levine on behalf of Drexel.

"After the close of the stock market on March 1, 1985, Coastal issued a press release revealing the terms of its tender offer for the stock of ANR."

On the basis of his knowledge—the closest a mortal can get to a sure thing—that the deal had a good chance of success, Levine purchased 145,500 shares of ANR from February 14 to March 1, 1985, at an average price per share of $49.93. When Coastal announced its intention to launch a tender offer, ANR's stock soared.

In a routine that was becoming as easy as buying a lottery ticket—and a lot more predictable than that—Levine sold his ANR shares on March 4, for a windfall profit of $1,370,610. Ironically, a day later Levine consented as an ANR director. Levine's Bank Leu portfolio manager, Bernhard Meier, who had slowly begun to raise his stakes, sold 2,000 shares for a profit of $24,518.

In the chain reaction that typifies insider trading, Meier used his information about the Coastal–ANR deal to introduce his boss, Bruno Pletscher, to the wonders of stock market leaks, and this introduction would help Pletscher offset recent losses from legitimate trading.

> *SEC:* "What was it that led you to open your securities trading account at Bank Leu International?"
> *Pletscher:* "My personal one?"
> *SEC:* "Yes?"
> *Pletscher:* "I opened my personal securities trading account upon discussions I had with Mr. Meier."
> *SEC:* "What was the substance of these discussions?"
> *Pletscher:* "Mr. Meier told me that he was doing some security transactions for his account and he said that there are certain opportunities that he feels I should benefit from as well and asked me why I do not have a security account. I then said that I do not feel safe trading in the stock market and that I cannot afford to lose money.
>
> "Mr. Meier then explained to me that there are certain new issues in the market that are very safe in the sense that there is an oversubscription and only a small portion of subscription is allocated, and that the public market usually opens at a higher price than the subscription price.
>
> "He showed me some of these new issues and said, 'This supports what I am saying, and I can allocate some of these to your account if you want to.' So this is the time when I was convinced that I should benefit from such occasions as well.
>
> "The next thing is that I got certain recommendation from Mr. Meier to participate in security trades. I remember that he came to me with an idea that was brought to his attention by a broker selling and buying OEX options, and he also showed me some figures of profits that he had already made. However, he also explained to me that these option trades have a certain

risk, and I said, 'I understand.' On the other hand, he said, 'Through these options you can make nice profits.' He recommended these options that I have participated in. He also recommended two or three security trades that I have participated in.

"Then there came the time that through these OEX options I lost about three thousand dollars. Mr. Meier then told me that he felt guilty for my losing the money. . . .

"I do not think it was the first time, but at that time he mentioned that I should participate in the trades that Mr. X is directing to us. He said to me, 'You must be aware of the fact that Mr. X has an excellent track record and that Mr. X had made a lot of profits.' He said, 'Why should not you also benefit from such trades? . . . Mr. X is investing in securities, and it happens that most of these trades are related to a takeover situation. This guy must know more than other people.' This sounded reasonable to me, and exciting, so I said, 'Let me know if you have the next deal coming up.' I said to Bernie, *'Mention only situations to me in which you feel comfortable and you expect a nice profit, because I cannot afford to lose money.'"*

"I remember that Mr. Meier then came to me and said, 'I have an order from Mr. X and you should participate in this one. This seems to be a good deal.' So I purchased five hundred ANR."

"I was very nervous about the investment and followed the price movements at least on an hourly basis, and about two or three days later Mr. Meier came to me and said, 'Bruno, you should increase your ANR. Why do you not buy another thousand? I have been told,' Mr. Meier said, *'this is a one-hundred-percent winner. Why do you not buy another thousand?'* I said, 'Another thousand? That is too much for me.' I said, 'I have already invested a lot of money.' Mr. Meier said, 'You can utilize the margin facility and borrow money

against the holdings you have.' I said, 'That is true.'
Then he said, 'Okay. Buy a thousand.' I said, 'No a
thousand is too much even with the margin facility.' He
said, 'Do not worry about the margin facility. This deal
comes through soon. You will make a nice profit and
your account will be clear.' So I hesitated and then
gave the order to buy another five hundred."

SEC: "When Mr. Meier first came to you, did he specifically
tell you that Mr. X was investing in ANR?"

Pletscher: "I think he did say that."

SEC: "Is that why you invested in ANR, because he specified ANR?"

Pletscher: "Yes, because prior to that he told me about Mr.
X's trades and his success in his dealings and said he
will come back to me when he has an order."

SEC: "When you were checking the price movements after
your initial purchase of five hundred shares, did you
notice any change before the time when Mr. Meier
came to you and suggested buying another one thousand shares?"

Pletscher: "As far as I remember there was a consistent upward trend. . . ."

SEC: "Do you remember whether Mr. Meier told you that
Mr. X said there was some sort of negotiation to acquire ANR going on?"

Pletscher: "I remember the statement that he said *'a one-
hundred-percent winner,'* but I cannot remember the
reasoning. . . ."

SEC: "Did your investment in ANR turn out to be profitable?"

Pletscher: "That is a slight understatement."

SEC: "Could you describe how profitable it was?"

Pletscher: "It was very profitable. *It was a joy to see the
figure.*"

Following up on his ANR coup, Levine turned 79,500 shares of McGraw-Edison (the object of a leveraged buyout) into profits of $906,836; 21,000 shares of Multimedia (leveraged buyout) into $129,460; 74,800 shares of Houston Natural Gas into $907,655; and 100,000 shares of Crown Zellerbach (a Sir James Goldsmith target) into gains of $82,334.

Like the Coastal deal, the Crown Zellerbach transaction provides revealing insight into Levine's access, as an investment banker, to confidential, nonpublic information on pending deals. In both cases, he was able to use his investment banking intelligence to trade in advance of the market.

In testimony to the SEC, Drexel's first vice-president, Douglas McClure, provided this bird's-eye view of Levine's involvement:

"In or about February 1985, I began to work on an investment financing transaction for Sir James Goldsmith and his affiliated companies. The purpose of the financing, which was then targeted to be in the $100 to $150 million range, was to make available to Goldsmith and his affiliated companies funds for the purpose of making investments in marketable securities in U.S. companies. At that time, no decision had been made on what those investments might be.

"On or about March 12, 1985, Sir James and his investment group filed with the SEC a schedule 13-D for their investment in Crown Zellerbach Corporation.

"During the last week of March 1985, I attended Drexel's high-yield bond conference which was held in Beverly Hills, California. This is an annual event involving presentations by high-yield bond issuers to institutional investors, and by guest speakers. Sir James Goldsmith was one of the speakers at the conference.

"While at the bond conference, I, along with two other Drexel employees [G. Chris Anderson and Dennis B. Levine], attended a meeting with Sir James to discuss his holdings in Crown Zellerbach, including but not necessarily limited to future strategy and tactics, financing, et cetera. The information provided to us by Sir James at the meeting was provided to Drexel in the strictest confidence."

Within days of the meeting, Levine instructed Bank Leu to purchase 50,000 shares of Crown Zellerbach stock for his account.

"During the remaining days of March 1985 and into April," McClure's account continues, "I along with Chris Anderson and Dennis Levine continued to work on the Crown transaction and both provided information to, and received information from, representatives of Sir James's investment group. Throughout this period, Mr. Levine had primary responsibility for the transaction from a merger-and-acquisition standpoint.

"On April 1, 1985, Dennis B. Levine, as managing director on behalf of Drexel, executed a 'highly confident' letter which was sent to Sir James Goldsmith at General Occidental Incorporated. Mr. Levine, on behalf of Drexel, subsequently executed a second 'highly confident' letter on or about April 9, 1985.

"On or about April 10, 1985, Sir James and his investment group announced and launched a cash tender offer for $42.50 a share for nearly 70 percent of the common stock of Crown."

But soon after Goldsmith's offer put Crown Zellerbach in play, Mead Corporation surfaced as a white knight, upping the ante for Crown's stock to $50 a share. Prompted by the prospect of a $7.50 sweetener over Goldsmith's bid, Levine got on the Bank Leu hotline, ordering an additional 50,000 shares of Crown stock. He would not hold the investment for long. To Levine's shock, word came quickly that Mead would be withdrawing its offer.

As Roland Franklin, a Goldsmith financial aide closely involved in the deal, recalled, news of Mead's cold feet sent shivers down Dennis's spine. The shock came at a meeting, held at Sir James's Manhattan townhouse, between Goldsmith's takeover team and a Mead representative.

SEC: "And who was present at that meeting?"
Franklin: "It was—the cast of characters at any particular moment in time I have difficulty recollecting, but during the day most of the people concerned were there. Dennis Levine was there. . . ."

SEC: "Could you describe what took place at the meeting?"

Franklin: "I arrived very shortly before the representative of Mead Corporation, who was their New York counsel, and he confirmed that Mead was considering, was in fact discussing with Crown Zellerbach making an offer for all shares at $50 a share and was asking whether we would cooperate, and we had extensive discussions with him on the terms of such cooperation. These went through till lunchtime. In the middle of lunch he was called by telephone and was told that Mead had terminated their interest in Crown Zellerbach."

SEC: "How did you learn, if at all, that Mead had terminated its interest in Crown Zellerbach?"

Franklin: "He came back from his telephone call and informed us. That was the source."

Asked how Dennis Levine, who was nearby, sitting with a big position in Crown stock, reacted to the news, Franklin put it this way: "I have a vivid recollection of it, because it was a matter subsequently of discussion between Goldsmith and myself, because when it was clear—when it was disclosed that the Mead deal was not going through—*it struck us both that Dennis Levine went gray;* and we both exchanged—we understand each other very well—we exchanged a look and we speculated at that time that he was deeply concerned that the deal was not going through, *and we speculated that he had a large number of shares or a number of shares and that was why he was concerned.* When the meeting broke up, Goldsmith said to me or I said to Goldsmith, in a lighthearted way, *we suspected that he was anxious to get to his broker as quickly as possible.*"

Panic-stricken is more like it. Holding 100,000 shares of Crown Zellerbach stock, Levine recognized a sinking ship when he saw one. He dashed to the nearest telephone and ordered Bank Leu to cash in his chips, posthaste. As usual, his Nassau-based cohorts followed suit.

SEC: "Mr. Pletscher, our review of your trading records indicates that on April 24, 1985, you purchased three hundred shares of a company called Crown Zellerbach Corporation and sold those . . . shares on April 25, 1985. Is that consistent with your recollection?"

Pletscher: "Yes."

SEC: "What was it that led you to purchase Crown Zellerbach?"

Pletscher: "This was a purchase that was made by Mr. X, and I recall the sale in particular. Mr. X called and said the deal is not going through and we should sell as quickly as possible. I was on the phone with Mr. X."

SEC: "You were on the phone when Mr. X said, 'The deal is going to fall through so sell as quickly as possible'?"

Pletscher: "Yes."

SEC: "Do you recall what led you to make the initial investment?"

Pletscher: "That was also a call from Mr. X, but I cannot recall any explanation why to buy. It was simply receiving an instruction from Mr. X to buy, and in this particular case I spoke to Mr. Meier, who was in Switzerland at that time, and asked him whether or not he wants to buy some Crown Zellerbach as well and that I have received an order from Mr. X to buy and that Mr. X said this is—I remember it now—'a short deal.' I also remember with Crown Zellerbach that he told us to buy as quickly as possible. The following day he informed me that the deal did not go through and I should sell as quickly as possible."

Less than twenty-four hours after the Levine ring sold their Crown holdings, Sir James canceled his tender offer for the company's stock. By learning of all the twists and turns before the market, and trading on that advance information, Levine was able to salvage what was by all measures an aborted deal, pocketing profits of $82,334.

*   *   *

In May of 1985, Levine hit the zenith of his Bank Leu trading spree, turning a 150,000-share stake in Nabisco Brands into profits of $2,694,421. The payoff came with the May 30 announcement from R. J. Reynolds that it was conducting merger talks with Nabisco, talks Levine learned about in advance through his now well-oiled trading ring.

In April 1985 Nabisco approached Levine's investment banking alma mater, Lehman Brothers, about a possible union with R. J. Reynolds. Although Dennis had since gone on to greener pastures at Drexel Burnham, his Lehman informant, Ira Sokolow, was engaged in round-the-clock surveillance. Alerted to the Nabisco–Reynolds deal through his work in the firm, Sokolow passed Levine nonpublic information about the negotiations, which continued from May 6 to May 21. During this time, Levine bought his Nabisco shares and tipped Boesky, who took a 377,000-share stake, producing a $4 million profit. As was now standard operating procedure, Levine's Bank Leu cohorts also piggybacked on the deal.

> *SEC:* "Our review of your account records indicates that you invested in a company called Nabisco Brands, purchasing three hundred shares on May 21, 1985, and selling those . . . shares on May 30, 1985. Is that consistent with your recollection?"
>
> *Pletscher:* "Yes."
>
> *SEC:* "What was it that led you to invest in Nabisco Brands?"
>
> *Pletscher:* "Mr. Meier told me that he has received an order from Mr. X and that he has received information from Mr. X that there is a takeover negotiation going on. Then I also got the indication on Nabisco, what Nabisco was doing with reference to the cookie business, and Mr. Meier told me that the information he got from Mr. X was that this is a takeover situation and should not take long."

With the Nabisco take added to his Bahamian stockpile, Levine added substantially to his trading profits—all tax-free and all safely ensconced in a secret bank account. But it wasn't enough. He would go on to trade until his "perfect crime" proved not so perfect after all. What drove this greed?

Rumor has it that Dennis's wife, Laurie—pictured by some as a Queens Boulevard girl with Madison Avenue tastes—was at the bottom of it. But those who knew the couple well say nothing could be farther from the truth.

"Some wives—the ones who are as eager as their spouses to acquire wealth and power and social position—wouldn't have died the same little death I'm sure Laurie died when her husband was branded a criminal on the front page of *The Wall Street Journal*," says a former Manhattan neighbor, who knew the couple socially and professionally. "Because the crown jewels of success are so important to these women, they push, they scheme, they encourage their husbands to cross into the gray areas of business ethics if that's what it takes to bring home the dollars.

"But Laurie wasn't like that. She never talked about money. Never wrapped herself in expensive clothes. Never acted like the nouveau riche she had become. Those who misread her may have been confused by her social skills. By the fact that she was the perfect corporate wife, attending Dennis's black-tie parties, small-talking with his colleagues and clients and, just like him, always having the right thing to say. But all of that sprang from a marvelously refreshing personality that always reminded me of a young and vivacious Lauren Bacall.

"There was nothing manipulative about her. A social climber? No way. Those who say Dennis did what he did to feed his wife's money habit didn't know either of them. The addiction to cars, artwork, statusy stuff—his name was written all over that.

"Maybe Dennis gave rise to the thinking that Laurie was behind the big spending. Now and then he'd hint around that his wife came from money, that her family had major bucks, some of which they'd showered on their beloved daughter.

"Why'd he cook that one up? I've thought about that a lot. The best I can tell is that he wanted to create an illusion. When people looked at the luxuries he was surrounding himself with, they'd say, 'That's okay. His wife's got money.'

"When [you] look back on it now, I guess Dennis thought he had all the angles covered."

He would soon find out that he didn't.

X

For Immediate Release

"*Dennis never liked me. That's what I've heard from others who were close to him. I think it's because in a merger deal, I require that the client appoint only one person to talk to the public and the press. This reduces the likelihood of leaks. Whoever is appointed to be the company spokesman—be it Joe Smith or Chaim Yunkel— becomes the filter through which all news, if there is to be any, flows. That's the way we operated on the Pantry Pride deal that Dennis was involved in—and he didn't like it. Perhaps he didn't want the leaks to stop.*"

—Takeover publicist GERSHON KEKST

When news of a takeover finally moves from the insider clique that has known about it for months to the investing public, it is delivered by another member of the M&A clan, the PR men. As managers of corporate news, these media manipulators play a dual role: to secure the lid of secrecy on pending deals and then, when the time is right, to lift that veil in a way that benefits their clients. But just when and how the information should be released can be the subject of debate within the takeover team. Takeover publicist Gershon Kekst found that out the first time he worked with Dennis Levine, on Pantry Pride's attack on Revlon.

Levine's concern that the leaks not be stopped suggests to some that he had taken a position in the Revlon stock that Pantry Pride's Ron Perelman was so hotly pursuing. But one of the interesting aspects of the deal is that, while this was one of the first takeovers for which Levine had managing responsibility, there is no evidence that he traded in the stock. This has led some of Levine's former colleagues to speculate that he may have had other, still undiscovered secret bank accounts. Some believe that Levine has another code-named account in Switzerland, larger than the Bank Leu account seized by the SEC.

To the PR men, including Kekst and his archrival Richard Cheney, chairman of the big PR firm Hill & Knowlton, takeovers are as much a battle for minds as for stock.

"In one takeover I worked on, it was discovered that the CEO of the target company was living with [his] mistress," Cheney recalls. "Because some of the people on the raider's team thought this would discredit management, they wanted us to take the story to the gossip magazines and create a scandal.

"But I advised against it. That the guy lived with [his] mistress didn't really matter. Not to the stockholders. Not unless the CEO was using company money to feather his lovenest. Then it would matter. And if he used a lot of money, and if the stock happened to be going down, and if the dividend was cut, well then, okay, it would matter a lot.

"But you can't use that kind of information on the strict ethics thing. No one cares. And they care less every day."

Not that all PR is negative. Ivan Boesky used public relations to enhance his career, hiring publicists, giving speeches and writing books—all in an effort to create an image of himself as a pillar of the financial community.

"Before Ivan came along, no one outside of Wall Street ever heard of arbitragers," says a senior Salomon Brothers executive. "Until then, it was a close-to-the-vest, hush-hush type of business. You did what you did, made your millions and kept quiet about it. That was the unspoken rule in arb land.

"To Boesky's way of thinking, that made sense for the established arb firms, but not for a newcomer trying to build a reputation and credibility on Wall Street. He believed that if he could use public relations to establish his image as a figure so critical to the financial community that people couldn't act without thinking about him or consulting with him, he'd be in the catbird's seat.

"The book he wrote, the magazine interviews he gave, the splashy donations he made—it was all a PR gambit and, if you think about it, one that worked. He got deals, he got attention, he got respect. Ivan was the first arb to hire PR men and it paid off for him in spades."

But who are these PR men? Why are they valued members of the M&A community? When do they learn of confidential information and how do they use it? How do they get started in the takeover business?

"When I first heard the word *takeover* I didn't know what the hell it was," says Kekst, who heads Kekst & Company, which, together with Hill & Knowlton and Adams & Rinehart, dominates M&A publicity. "But I learned fast. In the process, I discovered that takeovers are riddled with booby traps that you don't find in standard PR work."

A look at Kekst's career path, from the chaotic corridors of Ruder & Finn (a big New York PR firm that is said to be a revolving door for executive talent) to a money-minting takeover practice with his name on the door, underlines the incestuousness of the M&A business, revealing how members of an extended family cross paths in an interlocking grid of business and social relationships.

For Kekst, it all began with a favor from takeover ace Saul Steinberg. "One of my first takeover assignments surfaced when I was a senior vice-president with Ruder & Finn. My friend had sold his computer company to Saul Steinberg's Leasco Corporation, and he was instrumental in helping me land Leasco as a client.

"Later—after I'd done some substantial work for Leasco— Saul called me on the phone to tell me in confidence that he was planning one of the most brazen acts in American business history. Still in his twenties, only a few years out of Wharton, Steinberg was planning on taking over Chemical Bank, one of the bulwarks of the financial establishment.

"This was one of my first projects in the merger-and-acquisition business and I can't say that I handled it well. My critical mistake was in failing to see that the publicity requirements for a takeover are far different [from those] for promoting Coca-Cola. Takeovers demand a strategic, sharply focused approach, designed to win over the thinking of one or a few highly placed people—those critical to the transaction. In the case of Chemical Bank, that meant Chemical's CEO Bill Renchard and the bank's board of directors."

A starchy group—with more pride in their pedigrees than a litter of Irish wolfhounds—the Chemical men were likely to respond most favorably to a low-key approach that paid homage to the bank's long history and their place in it. Gentlemen doing business with gentlemen, was their style.

But the PR men lost sight of this. Employing the publicist's flair for drama and for spotlighting colorful personalities, the Ruder people, led by Kekst, played up the cultural gaps between Steinberg, the brash financial genius who had turned a Wharton thesis on IBM into a high-flying computer-leasing company (Leasco, now called Reliance Group) and the staid old bank he wanted to slip into his hip pocket. The image of the dynamic— not to mention arrogant and antagonistic—twenty-nine-year-old Jew from Long Island riding in to rescue Chemical from its sorry stewards prompted management and the board to rise up against him, bringing the whole weight of the WASP establishment crashing down on Steinberg. To quash the takeover, institutions holding Steinberg stock sold short massive amounts of Leasco shares, thus deflating the company's market value and its ability to acquire Chemical through an exchange of stock.

"I'm no psychiatrist, but it seems to me now that if the Chemical people were sleeping, the way we approached the thing forced them to wake up," admits Kekst, at first reticent to talk about his M&A activities, but warming to the subject once he gets started. "By making it an adversarial thing, we galvanized them and made it a lot harder to talk rationally about what Saul Steinberg had in mind."

In plotting media strategy for the then-secret Chemical take-over, Kekst sought to gain favorable treatment in *The New York Times* by making one of its reporters privy to Steinberg's plans. The idea was to include the journalist in Saul's inner circle. Once the story broke, the thinking went, Steinberg's plans for breathing new life into the bank would make headlines in the business section, thus gaining public (read "stockholder") support for the Steinberg camp.

But this too backfired. According to Kekst, the *Times* reporter took what he learned from the Steinberg powwows not to the newsroom, but instead directly to Renchard and the Chemical board. Incensed at what they heard (the Steinberg team is said to have considered the Chemical takeover a shoe-in), management and the board took Steinberg to the mat and beat him at his own game.

For the man considered by many the craftiest practitioner of takeover PR, the Chemical Bank fiasco was a learning experience, one that built bridges to the budding M&A community and that gave him entree to an explosive specialty when he left Ruder & Finn to start his own firm.

The parting came after years of haggling with Ruder & Finn's founders and chief executives, William Ruder and David Finn, over Kekst's clout in the firm. The central dispute is a familiar one in advertising and public relations agencies: it centered around the role of the rainmaker who reels in new clients versus the creative types who plan and implement the publicity campaigns. Kekst, a rainmaker if ever there was one, believed the Chinese wall between the functions should be dismantled, giving him some say in how his clients were serviced. But he couldn't sell the idea to the men who ran the agency.

Kekst's frustration with Ruder & Finn subsided when he was dispatched to California to spearhead the firm's West Coast expansion. Staying on to launch and manage branches in San Francisco, Los Angeles and Texas, the rebel in the ranks effectively ran his own show, putting his theories on client service and retention into play. But in the end, Kekst's stint on the West Coast made it intolerable for him to remain at the firm once he was called back to New York.

Walking out of Ruder & Finn's door and into the world of the unemployed, Kekst contemplated his options. There were offers for corporate jobs, but for a man who had built his career representing a wide mix of companies, being padlocked to a single client seemed more like a form of punishment than a career advancement. Invitations from other PR agencies were equally unattractive, but for a different reason. Though Ruder & Finn's competitors were bidding for his talents, Kekst recognized that going this route would just mean transporting his discontent from one firm to another. The agency that hired him as another Ed McMahon would view him solely as a salesman. He'd never be allowed to sit in Johnny's chair.

With all other options seemingly closed and with his term as Ruder & Finn's West Coast entrepreneur his most enjoyable experience at the firm, Kekst decided to open his own shop. Support for this approach came from a number of former clients in the M&A camp, including a ghost from the past.

"Before I left Ruder & Finn, I had a falling out with Saul Steinberg. He got angry [with] me and refused to talk to me again. So imagine how surprised I was when I took a call from Saul soon after I started Kekst & Company. The conversation, which surprised me even more, went like this:

"Saul: 'I heard you've started your own business. Is that true?'

"Kekst: 'Yes, it is.'

"Saul: 'Do you have enough money for your payroll, your rent?'

"Kekst: 'Yes, Saul, I do.'

"Saul: 'Good, but if you need help, call me.'" (Steinberg then hung up.)

"It was an abrupt call but it was the sweetest thing, coming as it did in a period of silence when if he saw me on the street he wouldn't even talk to me. Sometime after that surprise phone call, we patched up our differences and he's been a client ever since."

Support also came from another former client, Joe Flom. One of the pioneers in the M&A business, who built the law firm of Skadden Arps Slate Meagher & Flom from a legal lightweight to the preeminent takeover practice, Flom encouraged Kekst's budding entrepreneurship.

"From the moment he heard that I was thinking of leaving Ruder & Finn, Joe suggested that I go into business for myself," Kekst says. "Joe will tell you that he advised me to start my own agency, which is true. But he'll also tell you that he set me up in business, which is not true. He has told reporters that my first office was in his law library, but I've never even seen his law library. It wasn't until I was in business for about a year and a half or two years that he sent me clients."

It was worth the wait. When Flom's clients did come, they brought Kekst plum assignments that helped establish his reputation as the premier M&A publicist.

The turning point came with Kekst's campaign to protect Sterndent, a publicly traded supplier of dental equipment, from a hostile takeover. It was in the course of this deal that Kekst convinced even the most stubborn skeptics that PR played a critical role in takeovers.

The chess game began when a group of investors made a tender offer for Sterndent stock. Responding in typical fashion for besieged management, Sterndent hired Joe Flom to devise a legal defense for keeping the company independent. Flom, in turn, called in Kekst to handle the press. Together they dreamed up an outlandish but highly effective media campaign.

Convinced that the investor group wanted control of Sterndent for its inventory of gold bullion, which it sold to dentists for fillings, the takeover defense team turned to the consumers of that gold, the dental community, to roadblock the acquisition.

"We played on an emotional issue," Kekst says, "pointing out to the press that some of the members of the investor groups were Kuwaitis. Why do that? Because most of Sterndent's customers were dentists, and many dentists just happen to be Jewish. Clearly, Jews don't like to buy gold or other dental supplies from Arabs. So even though some of the members of the investment group were not Kuwaitis—a few, in fact, were American Jews— we kept labeling the raiders as an 'Arab investment group.'

"The prospect of an Arab-led takeover raised the hackles of some of the Jewish dentists, who took it upon themselves to write letters saying that if the Arabs acquired Sterndent, they'd switch to another supplier. We then distributed these letters to the press, who called the dentists and got the 'damn the Arabs' story we were looking for. In story after story, the dentists were quoted as saying they'd 'never buy a dime's worth of stuff from Sterndent if Arabs were going to profit.' It worked like a charm. In time the investment group grew uncomfortable—they didn't want that kind of notoriety and they feared the effects of a takeover on Sterndent's business. So they withdrew.

"The lawyer who represented the raiders dubbed our campaign the 'Jewish Dentists' Defense.' It put Kekst & Company on the map in M&A."

Interestingly, the Jewish issue crops up in the bad blood between Kekst and his chief rival in takeover PR, Hill & Knowlton's chairman, Dick Cheney. It is a rivalry that offers an interesting glimpse of PR people as insiders, privy to secret information on the very largest takeover plans of the industry's most noteworthy figures. In a chat with Cheney, the conversation drifts to a veiled charge that Kekst uses his "Jewishness" to lure clients away from Hill & Knowlton.

But to Kekst and others in the PR community Cheney's charges are the sour grapes of a man who has seen a former upstart replace him as number one in PR's most profitable market.

"Cheney used to be the guru everyone in M&A wanted on their side," says a principal in a small New York–based PR firm. "But somehow, in some way, Kekst has taken that role away from him. Now when companies want to acquire other companies or when they fear they themselves will be acquired, it's Kekst they turn to first.

"The raiders do the same. A whole pack of them have become bosom buddies with Kekst—a fact that hasn't sat well with Cheney. Losing Pickens was especially painful . . . and embarrassing."

T. Boone Pickens, Texas oil man, president of Mesa Petroleum, takeover artist extraordinaire and, to many, a financial genius in farmer's clothes was a client of Hill & Knowlton; he worked with Cheney through a duststorm of takeover activity including moves on Cities Service and Gulf Oil. But it was shortly after the Gulf deal that Pickens parted company with Hill & Knowlton, moving to the opposition, to Gershon Kekst, who had served as Gulf's PR man. Just why the switch occurred depends on which side one chooses to believe. Cheney blames it on an arrogant and ungrateful man who used his firm and then abandoned it.

"In the early days of the takeover business, the raiders used to think that the price they were offering for the company's stock should speak for itself," says Cheney, whose first M&A assignment was the 1960 battle for Alleghany Corp. "The feeling was that by talking a lot you only ran the risk of litigation and thus of ruining your deal. So PR was minimized. But as time went on, that changed.

"Pickens played a role in that change. Because he positioned himself as a man with a cause, fighting for the rights of the shareholders in getting greater value for their stock, he needed publicity to get his message across. So he decided he was going to take to the hustings. When it came to the Cities Service deal, I said, 'Let's have some fun with this.' I put him on TV, a cable show; that, I think, was his first television appearance. He warmed up to it immediately. He'd been trained for TV but he needed a lot more, so we worked with him on that.

"It progressed to the point that sometime during the Gulf deal, we said we'd like to put on our own electronic press conference—the first of its kind for a takeover. So we took Pickens over to our studio where the stations would call in and ask him questions and his answers would be taped for the evening news shows. But before we could get started, the truck bringing over the broadcast equipment had an accident on the East River Drive.

"Learning that, I went over personally to make sure everything went on track, to apologize for the delay and to explain—as if that were necessary—that the conditions causing the wreck were not under our control. But Pickens was contemptuous. I'd never seen anyone act like that before.

"He says, 'Come with me,' and heads for the men's room. It seemed that he had greasepaint on his face and wanted to wash it off. So he takes off his shirt, hands it to me and says, 'Hold this.' Well, let me tell you, I'm not afraid of anybody. It took great restraint not to throw that shirt in the toilet and tell him to get lost.

"Forget the press image we created for the man. That was the real Pickens in the studio that day. That 'I'm the friend of the stockholder' stuff, hah, he's the friend of Ivan Boesky, for Christ's sake. Not really, he's a friend of himself."

Gershon Kekst paints a radically different picture. "It was soon after the Gulf fight that Pickens's secretary called and said he'd like to meet me. I thought that would be very nice so we met and talked about the possibility of doing business together. At first I told Boone I couldn't afford a relationship with him. 'Think of all the deals I got because you were on the other side,' I said. 'If I work for you, I'll lose all that business in the future.' We sort of haggled about that for a while but ultimately came up with an arrangement acceptable to both of us. I could continue to represent any existing clients that he might develop an appetite for, but on anything else I'd work for Boone. I guess Dick Cheney took that very hard.

"Pickens is a tough and intelligent man with a natural instinct—like that of a skilled politician—for the public and the press. The last thing he needs is help in getting publicity. So if you're a big PR firm like Hill & Knowlton and you assign two or three or four people to be the press department for Pickens, you are just putting stumbling blocks in his way. Assigning some fifth-year PR associate to brief Boone Pickens on how to talk to Bob Cole of *The New York Times* is just dumb. All he needs is an objective view of what he's talking about and how he's coming off. A critical devil's advocacy. That's what he wanted and that's why he's here with us."

The Pickens coup pleased Kekst not only because it put another rich and famous M&A client on retainer, but also because it proved that Jewishness had nothing to do with his success. (Pickens may not be Jewish, but it depends on how you define "Jewish." Says one Wall Street insider who also lists the oil man as a client: "Boone may be an elder of the church but he's more Jewish than a lot of Jews. It's in the way he thinks. We all kid him about it.")

"Clients who hired me after being Hill & Knowlton clients

were not, with one exception, Jewish people. Boone Pickens certainly isn't Jewish. No one at Transamerica is Jewish. Nobody at Bank America is Jewish."

Different though their styles and approaches may be, the top takeover publicists and their staffs have one thing in common. They learn of pending deals before they are made public; they are privy to a babbling brook of inside information.

As Dick Cheney learned some years ago, that can be dangerous—if one bends to the temptations.

Cheney's baptism in the M&A fires came at the side of attorney George Demas, the sole practitioner who, along with Joe Flom, handled most of the proxy battles of the 1950s and early 1960s. Before the two lawyers went at each other in the snake pit (the room where the proxies were counted and where both sides argued over their validity), the PR men—including Cheney, who worked for Demas on about a dozen deals—wrote letters trying to sway the stockholders and the press to their client's side.

Although Cheney went on to handle PR for a Who's Who of M&A players, he continued to work with Demas and subsequently for Demas's law partner and son-in-law, Dave Hall.

"When George left active practice to pursue real estate investments in the Caribbean, Dave, who was married and then divorced from George's daughter, stayed in New York to run the firm," recalls Cheney, whose large, tastelessly furnished office looks out over the top of Grand Central Station. "He did small deals, proxy fights and the like, and I worked on many of them with him.

"Well, one day I get this shocking call from Dave, who blurts out, 'They got me!' When I asked who the 'they' was, he said, 'The SEC.' It seemed he'd traded on client information and was going to jail for it. I would have thought he'd have more sense than that. Inside trading is something professionals just can't engage in—and can't tolerate in their firms."

*   *   *

But has Dick Cheney taken meaningful steps to prevent inside trading at Hill & Knowlton? Has Kekst at his firm? The PR men, whose clients tip them off to secret information while it can still bring millions in stock market profits, have installed only limited controls to prevent abuse of this privilege within their respected domains.

"The big PR firms have hundreds of people running around, writing and dictating and typing press releases about corporate transactions that are still, as far as most of the world is concerned, secret," comments an M&A lawyer who has worked with all the top takeover publicists.

"Let's say, for example, that Smith Metal Bending aims to swallow up Jones Iron Ore. Smith's CEO contacts a PR firm, whose president cheerfully accepts the assignment. But he doesn't really do anything for the client. That's why he has this enormous staff on the payroll. First he calls in a shiny young account executive—make that two account executives if it's a big enough piece of business—to hold the client's hand. Instantly, these people are informed that Smith is making eyes at Jones.

"But that's only the beginning. Next the writers are called in, followed by the media experts and the stockholder relations people and the proxy counters. [Some leading PR firms, such as Hill & Knowlton, have their own proxy department.] And on and on. Add to this so-called professional staff, the secretaries, the clerks, the typists, the proofreaders, and don't forget the guy who runs the copying machine. All told, a hundred people may know what's supposed to be a deep, dark secret.

"I don't care if the firm uses code names, sign language or invisible ink to keep these secrets secret. With so many cooks stirring the soup, people are going to find out what's happening and some of them are going to trade on it."

"The clerks, the typists, the proofreaders, and don't forget the guy who runs the copying machine"—a prophetic statement when a case in the next chapter is considered. For here is another class of insider, one perhaps less high-flying, than the headline makers—but just as effective.

XI

Reading Between the Lines

"*Our era aptly has been styled, and well may be remembered as, the 'age of information.' Francis Bacon recognized nearly four hundred years ago that 'knowledge is power,' but only in the last generation has it risen to the equivalent of the coin of the realm. Nowhere is this commodity more valuable or volatile than in the world of high finance, where facts worth fortunes while secret may be rendered worthless once revealed.*"
—JUDGE IRVING KAUFMAN, *U.S. Court of Appeals, Second Circuit*

Inside trading is not a rich man's sport. In spite of front-page headlines linking Wall Street luminary Ivan Boesky and rising star Dennis Levine to the granddaddy of trading schemes, the rogue's gallery of convicted traders is filled with more nobodies than household names, more nine-to-fivers than financial wunderkinds.

The truth is that although the stock exchanges, the SEC and the assorted watchdogs of the securities market prefer to play this down, insider trading is a game for the masses. Insiders at all levels aspire to play; many who have the opportunity do. Unlike robbing a bank or stealing a car, insider trading is not generally viewed as a crime.

Instead it is seen as a chance to make a killing, to claim the same advantage the rich and well-connected have enjoyed for years. That's what brings the word processors, the office managers, the proofreaders, the receptionists, the secretaries and the cab drivers into the world of illegal trades—and that's what will keep them at it as long as there is information to be learned and fast money to be made.

It worked that way for a proofreader at Bowne & Co., one of the big Wall Street printing shops that churns out the snowstorm of corporate reports, proxy solicitations and tender materials that go hand in hand with corporate restructurings. Though they are clearly outside the takeover team, the financial printers are nevertheless permanent fixtures along the chain of information that relays word of pending transactions to a network of insiders.

In a typical case, news of an evolving tender offer moves from the acquirer to the investment banker, then to the lawyer who prepares the tender offer, and then to the financial printer who prints the documents. Because the paperwork must be prepared before the offer is announced, the printer learns of the deal well in advance of the tender date. This widens the circle of insiders beyond those involved in shaping the transaction—who have a professional obligation to keep it secret—to those simply servicing the active participants in the deal. To this second sphere of insiders, learning of a secret deal is like eavesdropping on a party line: bad manners, but you don't get rich minding your etiquette.

Exactly the way Bowne proofreader Anthony Materia felt. A nickel-and-dime stock market speculator for most of his life, the self-described "stockaholic" would beeline from his night-shift job at the printing firm, arriving early in the morning at the Brooklyn brokerage offices of Josephthal & Co., where he maintained an account and where he would watch the tape as if hypnotized by the parade of symbols and numbers. Materia surrounded himself with investment paraphernalia; his apartment was cluttered with analyst reports, market letters and earnings statements. He would try systems, formulas, everything short of rabbit's feet to hit the next Xerox, the next solid-gold stock that would take him out of Bowne, out of Brooklyn, into the life of affluence he dreamed about.

And then he found a way, the only sure way, to win in the market—inside information. With reports on dozens of "secret" deals pouring into Bowne at any given time, learning which corporations were involved and what they were planning would be a piece of cake. For a man determined to make a killing in the market there could be no better place to work.

Federal judge Irving Kaufman notes: "At a certain point, amorphous data must be translated into the written word. In the financial field, this transmogrification requires masses of information—much of it highly sensitive—to be channeled through the financial printing firms that service our great commercial centers. It was in one such firm that Anthony Materia worked. Materia stole information to which he was privy in his work and traded on that information to his pecuniary advantage."

In one case, PC Industries, a subsidiary of the Manhattan-based investment company Dyson-Kissner-Moran, decided in the summer of 1982 to make a bid for Criton, a manufacturing company headquartered in Bellevue, Washington. Initiating the take-over, Dyson hired the M&A legal firm Wachtell, Lipton, which in turn commissioned Bowne to print the tender-offer materials. On August 14 a Wachtell, Lipton lawyer dispatched to Bowne the initial draft of PCI's offer to purchase.

With the document now in house at Bowne, two safeguards that are standard with financial printers were supposed to prevent word of the proposed tender from walking out the door at night. First, Bowne maintained a written policy on the confidentiality of customer information, prohibiting, among other things, copying documents or removing them from Bowne's offices. The policy also advised employees of insider trading laws and described the civil and criminal penalties that could result for engaging in such conduct. All of this was kept on permanent display on a bulletin board above the company's time clocks.

Second, names of the target companies were routinely omitted from the draft documents to stymie those inclined to trade on advance news of client transactions. They would know that a tender offer was in the making, but they would not know—at least in theory—whose stock would be tendered. Without that critical piece of the puzzle, the rest of the information would be useless.

But like most of the checks and balances built into the system, Bowne's were less than effective deterrents. A sign posted on a bulletin board may be a convenient way to discharge a company's responsibility vis-à-vis insider trading, but it does little to discourage a dishonest employee from breaking the rules. In the same vein, omitting the target company's name from the offering documents is less of a critical blank than would it first appear. With the document providing a wealth of descriptive information about the company, even third-rate sleuths can uncover the identity of the target.

Such was the case when an offering document for shares of

Evans-Aristocrat Industries, Inc., came into Bowne. Though the target's name was left out, the names of its operating divisions, Evans Rule and Aristocrat Leather, were there to behold in black and white. It didn't take a Sherlock Holmes to make the connection. After a careful review of the documents, Materia purchased 9,000 shares of Evans-Aristocrat Industries.

Judge Kaufman recounts: "Materia was employed by Bowne . . . of New York City, a firm specializing in the printing of financial documents, including many used by its corporate clients in connection with proposed tender offers. Because even a hint of an upcoming tender offer may send the price of the target company's stock soaring, information regarding the identity of a target is extremely sensitive and zealously guarded. It is customary, therefore, for offerors (or their law firms, which ordinarily draft such documents) to omit information that might tend to identify a target company until the last possible moment. Code names are used, blanks are left to be filled in on the eve of publication, and occasionally misinformation is even included in early drafts. In sum, a quick reading of preliminary versions of these sensitive papers would not reveal the information sought to be guarded.

"Anthony Materia did not read such material quickly. In his job as a copyholder, Materia read clients' drafts aloud to a proofreader, who in turn checked to make certain that page proofs conformed to the copy received from the client. If copyholding was Materia's vocation, the stock market appears to have been equally consuming. Notwithstanding efforts by Bowne and its clients to keep confidential information confidential, Materia was able to divine the identities of at least four tender-offer targets in the period between December 1980 and September 1982. Within hours of each discovery he purchased stock, and within days— after the offer had been made public—he sold his holdings at substantial gains."

In the Criton case, the offer to purchase, or OTP, which dutifully omitted Criton's name, drew a revealing profile of the company, listing this grab-bag of clues:

- state of incorporation

- number of outstanding shares

- price range of shares

- dividends paid

- information that the shares traded on the New York Stock Exchange

- business address

- description of business

- selected consolidated summary financial information

If that was not enough to turn an observer into an insider, the target company's telephone number was listed. An effort to delete this was made by drawing a line through it with a pencil.

On August 19, 1982, a day after receiving the OTP draft from Wachtell, Lipton, Bowne put the document into production— thirty copies for the client and ten to twelve for internal use within the printing firm. On August 23 Bowne received a revised draft of the OTP proof, this time identifying Criton as the target company. Again, thirty copies were printed for the law firm, ten to twelve for internal use. A day later, PC Industries announced its tender offer for Criton.

While the documents were being proofed and printed, Materia, who had access to them, was busy buying Criton stock. Leaving his Bowne shift at 9:00 A.M. on the morning of August 20, he placed an order through Fidelity Brokerage Services for 2,000 Criton shares at $30 each. Shortly before noon that day, he struck again, buying another 1,000 shares at $30⅞.

And then, in a pattern common with inside traders, he began to spread the wealth, building a trading ring of his own. The same day that Materia purchased his Criton shares, Fidelity received a telephone call (placed from a Brooklyn pay phone) from an elderly man (who turned out to be Materia's friend) who wanted to place an order for Criton stock. With the Fidelity clerk on the line, the caller—whose order was being routinely tape-recorded—paused to ask a companion, "Is it supposed to happen today or Monday?" Quickly the companion responded, "After the close today." With that the caller purchased 100 Criton shares. As it turned out, the companion's voice was that of Anthony Materia.

"The tape, which turned up after the case was in court, turned out to be a trial attorney's dream," says SEC attorney Anne Flannery, who handled the case. "Until that point, Materia claimed he had no knowledge of the various market developments. The recording contradicted that in open court."

But Materia's tips weren't limited to a single acquaintance. Relatives went on to buy thousands of Criton shares before the tender offer was made public. Before his trading gambit came to an end, Materia traded in stocks of Buffalo Forge (which was sought after by Bowne client Ampco-Pittsburgh); Brookwood Health Services, Inc. (sought after by Bowne client Humana Inc.); and Cenco, Inc. (the Bowne client was National Medical Enterprises, Inc.). His profits reached a total of $99,862. A substantial take for any investor, a virtual sweepstakes for a middle-aged union man from Brooklyn.

While a small-change operator like Anthony Materia appears insignificant viewed in the context of subsequent schemes, the case produced a landmark court decision that actually paved the way for nailing Dennis Levine and in turn Ivan Boesky.

Three years before the Materia action, the U.S. Attorney had failed in its attempt to prosecute another financial printer's employee, Vincent Chiarella, who worked in a composing room at New York's Pandick Press. (But Chiarella consented to a civil injunction brought by the SEC, and agreed to disgorge specified financial gains.) As with Materia, the government alleged that Chiarella used information gleaned from confidential documents to buy stock in takeover candidates. In one instance, according to the SEC, Chiarella learned on November 9, 1976, that General Cable Corporation was on the verge of tendering for the stock of Sprague Electric Company. The next day, he allegedly purchased 2,200 Sprague shares. Less than a week later—after the tender offer was announced—Chiarella sold his shares for a profit of $16,138.

In taking Chiarella to court, the U.S. Attorney's Office based its argument on the straightforward premise that the Pandick employee had violated the securities laws by trading on confidential, nonpublic information. While Chiarella was convicted in the District Court of New York, the decision was overturned by the Supreme Court on the grounds that Chiarella did not have a "relationship of trust and confidence" with the other stockholders from whom he bought his shares.

In effect, the court was saying that simply knowing a secret and trading on it was not necessarily a violation of the law unless a person had a "relationship of trust and confidence" with the stockholders, as a corporate executive or director might have. This seemed to leave a gaping hole in the government's efforts to prosecute the widening spectrum of inside traders, since only classic insiders within the ranks of corporate management would have such a relationship with stockholders. But the court left open a solution to the problem.

Writing a dissenting opinion in the Chiarella case, Chief Justice Warren Burger contended that Chiarella had indeed violated the securities laws by breaking a responsibility—not to stockholders, with whom he clearly had no relationship—but instead to his employer, who was bound to maintain the secrecy of its clients' affairs. This reasoning, which was soon backed by the New York Federal Appeals Court in the criminal case of Morgan Stanley securities trader James Newman, became known as the "misappropriation theory." In effect, it held that culpability for inside trading did not hinge on a duty to the stockholders but could be based on a responsibility to the trader's employer.

But to this point, the high-court test on misappropriation was limited to criminal cases. Whether the SEC could use the theory for civil prosecutions was uncertain until the Materia case.

"The Supreme Court's refusal to hear Materia's appeal, thus letting his conviction in the circuit court stand, was a landmark because it showed that the misappropriation theory could be applied to civil as well as criminal cases," says SEC trial attorney Anne Flannery. "It established, for the first time, that the SEC could win insider trading cases on the basis of the misappropriation theory.

"Because it was proven that Materia had a fiduciary responsibility to keep the information he learned at Bowne confidential, and because he violated that responsibility, he was found liable under the misappropriation theory. This gave us the legal ammunition to prosecute the likes of a Dennis Levine. Clearly, Levine had a similar responsibility to his employer. When clients informed Smith Barney, Lehman or Drexel that they were going after ABC, EFG or XYZ companies, that information was entrusted to the investment banks. Levine was duty-bound to limit the use of that information to his professional activities. That he went beyond that—misappropriating his client's confidence for personal gain—was clearly a violation of the securities laws."

But what of those with no responsibility to the stockholders, to their employers or to anyone else. What of those who are simply tipped off to inside information by those who misappropriate it?

In landmark case, *Dirks* v. *Equity Funding*, the Supreme Court held that an individual (the tippee) can be held liable for taking information from another person (the tipper) if he knows that information is material and nonpublic and that the tipper breached a fiduciary responsibility in passing the information on to him. In effect, the securities laws extend not only to those who misappropriate information (the tippers) but also to those they tell (the tippees) about it. This cleared the way for prosecuting individuals who are tipped off by insiders even if the informants had no fiduciary responsibility to keep the information confidential.

"The Dirks case established that if you can show that the tippee knew the information was material and nonpublic, that the tipper breached a duty in passing it to another party, and that the tipper gained direct or indirect benefit from releasing the infor-

mation, then you have culpability on the part of the tippees,"
Flannery says. "That's what enabled the government to build a
case against the Yuppie Five and subsequently against Ivan
Boesky."

That he had no fiduciary responsibility—something that might
have given Boesky a false sense of security—didn't mean a
thing.

An investment banker who believes that a string of arbs is
likely to fall victim to the tippee rule comments: "This is the one
that has the arbs—and I'm talking about some very big names
here—counting sheep at night. Before the recent cases really
brought the tippee rule to light and showed that the SEC would
be aggressive in using it, the arbs thought that they were immune
because they weren't classic insiders. But by rewriting the rules,
by saying that profiting from an insider is the same thing as being
an insider, the courts have created a fat strip of flypaper that's
going to catch some of these guys in the act.

"When I saw a prominent arb at a sporting event the other day,
I thought to myself, maybe next year he'll be watching it from the
prison library."

XII

The Fall

"The one thing Levine didn't account for is greed. He failed to recognize that once he started picking perfect stocks time and again, others would piggyback on his trades. While he couldn't have known that would lead to an anonymous letter from Caracas, Venezuela, he should have known that something was bound to happen—that he couldn't keep what he was doing to himself. Greed makes that impossible. It was naive not to recognize that."

—CHARLES CARBERRY,
Chief of the Securities and Commodities Fraud Unit,
U.S. Attorney's Office for the Southern District of New York

On a quiet morning in May 1985, a bombshell delivered to Merrill Lynch's New York offices would spell the beginning of the end of the Dennis Levine–Ivan Boesky trading scheme.

In a one-page letter, postmarked Caracas, Venezuela, an anonymous source charged brokers in Merrill Lynch's Caracas office with trading on inside information. Written in broken English on a manual typewriter, the letter alerted the Merrill Lynch compliance department to a trading triangle that stretched from New York to Caracas to Nassau. But it would be nearly another year before the name of Dennis Levine would surface as the mastermind behind it all, and another six months still before the Boesky connection would emerge.

"Even though the anonymous letter offered no evidence of the Caracas brokers' activities—there were no dates, no stocks, no dollar amounts—we launched an investigation, as is routine practice with all such charges," says Bob Romano, then a Merrill Lynch attorney responsible for SEC compliance. "One of our investigators started by looking into the brokers' accounts."

It didn't take long to confirm that the anonymous letter was on to something. In a series of miraculously prescient trades, the brokers allegedly purchased shares immediately preceding takeovers, leveraged buyouts and other M&A transactions; sold as soon as news of the deals became public; and banked handsome gains with stunning regularity. Questioned about this Hall of Fame hitting streak, the Merrill Lynch brokers reportedly led the firm's investigators to one of its former brokers in New York, who had counted Bank Leu among his major customers. The plot thickened when Merrill Lynch discovered that Bank Leu had bought many of the same takeover stocks as the Merrill Lynch reps.

"Because the Bahamian orders preceded those of the brokers," Romano recounts, "we deduced that the source of insider leaks had to be tied to Bank Leu."

Aware that the SEC was already investigating suspicious pre-announcement run-ups in such stocks as Carter Hawley Hale and the Jewel Companies—both of which were bought by Bank Leu—Romano, with the Merrill Lynch investigative report in hand, called the SEC in June to unload a bombshell of his own, telling of the anonymous letter and the suspicious trading pattern.

"I spoke first with Gary Lynch and John Sturc, and they were clearly excited by what I had to say," Romano recalls. "In any case, they called me back within twenty-four hours, wanting to know everything I could tell them about the anonymous letter, and what our internal investigation had uncovered."

Stirred by Merrill Lynch's findings, the SEC launched a full-scale investigation, training its sights on twenty-seven suspicious stocks in Bank Leu's trading accounts. Long aware that insiders were turning profits on a series of takeover announcements, the Feds were searching far and wide for a unifying element that would tie together the trading anomalies in dozens of stocks. Merrill Lynch's investigation appeared to be the breakthrough they had been looking for.

"It was as if the SEC had been playing with the Rubik's Cube of the Levine–Boesky case for years, trying all the combinations but the right one," says a participant in Merrill's in-house probe. "Then we came along and supplied the missing link. Suddenly the puzzle went click."

Armed with its hot list of suspicious stocks, the SEC took its attack public, pressing Bank Leu for full and immediate disclosure. Bruno Pletscher recalled learning of the government's surprise offensive from a dazed and slightly delirious Bernhard Meier.

SEC: "Mr. Pletscher, when did you first learn of the existence of the SEC investigation in the matter of Bank Leu?"

Pletscher: "In the late summer of 1985 there were two or three situations that happened concurrently, and those were a copy information that we got from our head office in Zurich, Bank Leu, Limited; also a telecopy information received from the SEC; and also a telephone call that Mr. Meier received from the SEC. These three events happened more or less at the same time, if not the same day, and Mr. Meier advised me accordingly."

SEC: "Can you give an approximate date when these events occurred?"

Pletscher: "It was around the end of August or beginning of September."

SEC: "1985?"

Pletscher: "1985."

SEC: "What was the nature of the information that you received from the head office?"

Pletscher: "The nature was that a broker at the head office has received an inquiry from the SEC and it was mentioned that it is in respect of the trading of Bank Leu International."

SEC: "Were particular trades identified?"

Pletscher: "To the best of my recollection, there were twenty-seven items mentioned in this inquiry."

SEC: "Did those twenty-seven items relate to the trading of a particular customer of yours?"

Pletscher: "When Mr. Meier referred these messages to me, he pointed out that these are trades of Mr. X's."

SEC: "The telephone call that was received from the SEC— did you say it was by Mr. Meier?"

Pletscher: "Yes."

SEC: "What was the general nature of the call?"

Pletscher: "The general nature of that call, as far as it was brought to my attention, was that the SEC has started an inquiry and wants to know a lot of things about our trading and details of tradings within the twenty-seven items listed. Mr. Meier told me that the SEC expects a response from our side of what we are going to do."

SEC: "What did you or Mr. Meier do in reaction to that SEC phone call?"

Pletscher: "As a reaction at the time, Mr. Meier came to my office. He was very angry and pointed out that it was in relation to the trades of Mr. X. *He pointed out that we are in the 'shit.'*"

Stunned and shaken by the SEC probe, the two bankers, who had grown accustomed to a Disney World life of crystal-ball stock tips and magic-wand profits, turned to their newfound Svengali for a way out of the "shit" they were now deeply embedded in. Unable to call Levine—he had always kept his telephone number under wraps—Pletscher and Meier waited impatiently for the mystery man to dial them, as was his practice at least once a week.

When the call came through, Meier pounced on Levine, alerting him to the SEC investigation and pleading that he come to Nassau immediately. A paragon of cool, Levine assured Meier that there was nothing at all to fret about and promised to come to the bank shortly. True to his word, he arrived at the Nassau branch within days of the call. His objective? To set the wheels in motion on a complex cover-up designed to camouflage his illegal trading and to stymie the SEC investigation. The unflappable Levine did not know at the time that his cover-up plan would lead ultimately to his unmasking.

The foil was carefully calculated to convince the SEC that Bank Leu, rather than the owner of the account (whose identity was still protected by Bahamian secrecy laws), made the investment decisions for Mr. Diamond. If Pletscher, Meier et al. could demonstrate convincingly that they picked Nabisco, Jewel, Carter

Hawley Hale and all other stocks on the basis of favorable news reports and brokerage analyses, the investigation would be stopped in its tracks. Absent the scent of inside trading, the SEC's bloodhounds would retreat, leaving Levine and his cohorts to resume their stock market sweepstakes.

Convinced that the SEC was a naive and ignorant bureaucracy, Levine believed he could lie and have it believed as gospel. After all, hadn't they let him wiggle out of their net earlier in the Textron case, swallowing lies a grade-schooler would see through? Hadn't he proved more times than he could count on both hands that he could beat the system? Couldn't he do it again?

Huddled with his shaken bankers days after the SEC letter threw ice water on their tropical paradise, Levine concocted his second SEC cover-up.

SEC: "Did you meet with Mr. X?"

Pletscher: "Yes. Mr. X came within the same week."

SEC: "What week was that approximately?"

Pletscher: "It is the first week in September. Mr. Meier showed him the letter we got from the SEC. I was also attending the meeting. Mr. X said, *'That is no problem. We can deal with this matter.'*"

SEC: "Mr. X said, 'We can deal with this.' What else did he say?"

Pletscher: "He said, 'Do you have a lot of managed portfolios? It could be possible to have such trades within your managed portfolios.' We said, 'Yes, but this is not a managed portfolio.' Mr. X said, 'The SEC does not know that, and if you go to the SEC and tell them that you have traded in these stocks on behalf of your managed portfolios, you are the smart guys; you have decided to buy these securities and allocate them throughout your portfolios; the SEC cannot prove the opposite.'"

SEC: "Is it a fact that all of his trades were in a nonmanaged portfolio?"

Pletscher: "That is correct."

SEC: "Was there any discussion at that meeting about obtaining counsel for the bank?"

Pletscher: "Yes. We asked Mr. X whether or not it would be advisable to have counsel representing us, vis-à-vis the SEC, since this is in a different jurisdiction and this is a legal matter. He said yes, most certainly, and he would recommend that we take the best. We then said, 'We do not have any connection with counsel that would be appropriate to deal in SEC matters.' He then said he has knowledge and he knows the lawyers that would be the best for this case, and he said the best to his knowledge is Harvey Pitt of Fried, Frank and . . . if Mr. Pitt would represent our case in saying that we have everything done through managed portfolios, then we should not have a problem in solving this matter pretty soon."

SEC: "Are you saying that he advised you to inform any lawyer that you would retain that the trading was through managed accounts?"

Pletscher: "He said that we should refer the message to the lawyer that we have all managed portfolios, that we have made the decisions, and to tell the lawyer all the facts that we have that led to the decision of buying these securities. The lawyers then would pass on this message and pass on what they learned from us to the SEC and we should not have any further problems."

SEC: "You mentioned before that he suggested you tell the SEC that the trading was done in managed accounts and that you—and I assume that meant you and/or Mr. Meier—had made the investment decision with respect to the securities for the managed accounts. Was there any discussion as to providing an explanation or a basis for why the investment decisions were made by you or Mr. Meier for the managed accounts?"

Pletscher: "Yes. Mr. X went on and covered all the parts of this plan. As a response to my remark that his account is not a managed account, he said we can arrange to have this paper signed in order to show his file also as a managed portfolio and, furthermore, that he could supply us with sufficient information so that the decisions to buy these shares were possible and justified by us."

SEC: "Did he identify what type of information he was going to look for?"

Pletscher: "He said he is looking for newspaper clippings, brokers' reports and other public information that was available prior to the investment decisions."

Convinced that he could hoodwink the SEC into believing that Bank Leu acted on its own, without the benefit of inside information, in buying the twenty-seven stocks, Levine prepared investment rationale for each of the stocks. This was passed on by the bankers to the Fried, Frank law firm.

PRIVILEGED AND CONFIDENTIAL, COMMUNICATION TO COUNSEL, ATTORNEY WORK PRODUCT

JEWEL COMPANIES

26.3.84   *Initial position*
           As the trading chart shows I bought initially 10,000 shs. at prices between $43.50 and $44.125.

30.3.84   *Increased position/averaged up*
           All the brokers I initiated positions with kept me up to date on rumors and stock price moves (Europartners, Kidder, Merrill, Dean Witter, Pru Bache). I bought another 11,000 shs. at prices between $48.125 to $48.375.

Rumors had already started about a possible leveraged buyout and prices mentioned were between $65 to $75 per share; the stock started to trade much more actively.

26.4.84   *Further increase in my position*
I bought 46,000 shs. at prices between $49 to $49.50. I was encouraged by the stock price action, heavier volume and lots of talk about the company.

31.5.84   *Further increase in my position*
I bought 24,900 shs. at prices between $51.50 to $53.50. Over $50 the stock seemed to get costly especially if there would be no deal. The volume on the stock and the way the stock traded (blocks on up-ticks) led me to believe that there was something going on.

6.6.84   *Balance of the position*
I bought 1,000 shs. at $66 and 2,000 shs. at $63. Pure arbitrage for a few points. As I had done on 9.5.84 with 1,400 shs. which I day-traded, bought at $51.5/$51.375, sold at $65.

CARTER HAWLEY (retail department stores; sixth largest department store chain)
(Other dept. stores: Allied stores, dry goods, Federated, Sears, Macys, May Dept. Stores, K. Mart, Dayton Hudson)

Department stores	Broadway–Southern California
	Broadway–Southwest
	Emporium Capwell
	*Thalhimers
	*John Wanamaker
High Fashion	Bergdorf Goodman
	·Nieman Marcus
Specialized merchandising	Contempo Casuals
	·Waldenbooks

*dogs
·stars

This company had good earnings gains in 1984 (financial year ends January)—1983 $1.55/1984 $1.93—and strong sales gains—a turnaround situation. CHH had three unsatisfactory years behind and could finally show strong sales gains and increased earnings.

Earnings prospects looked very promising for 1984/85 ('84, 2.60–2.70; '85, 3.10–3.70) also due to better cost controls. The P/E on the stock was relatively low (1) within the group and (2) considering the projected earnings growth for the coming years.

In addition, we heard some rumors out of Europe that BAT Industries, a British company, could be looking at CHH (BAT acquired Marshall Field's in 1982). The stock started to trade very actively and I decided to increase my position.

CROWN ZELLERBACH (forest products)

Good asset play. Sir James Goldsmith was involved before (CCC and St. Regis) and according to his reputation he seeks control and liquidates his acquisitions for the real value of their assets.

ZB owned 2 million acres of timber land besides other substantial assets; the timber land was valued at $45 to $50 a share by analysts.

Goldsmith filed and expressed his intention to raise his position to 25% but had not made a decision whether to seek control.

ZB took some anti-takeover measures ("poison pill") which were claimed to be destructive of the best interest of shareholders.

There was also a good possibility for a "white knight" third party stepping in.

Since the company was very open about their dislike for Mr. Goldsmith I could imagine that the company was probably looking themselves to find somebody who would be interested to buy ZB on a more friendly basis. In the takeovers management seems to be always concerned about keeping their jobs and I am almost sure if Goldsmith would have gotten control he would have liked to see some of his own people on top of the company.

Why did we sell: stock started to weaken on volume—I decided to reduce exposure. I continued to hold a position which I decided to sell on May 1, 1985.

Crown Zellerbach was recommended at the time by various brokers as a speculative buy for a takeover.

NABISCO BRANDS

As you all know, this view was shared by the U.S. and other governments.

All these factors combined would affect the future prosperity of Nabisco in a major way; therefore the outlook for NB into the 2nd half of 1985 and 1986 was extremely bright, and I may add that in addition NB's constant efforts to increase their market shares, improve their product mix, increase the manufacturing efficiency etc., were additional positive attributes which encouraged me to buy the stock.

SUMMARY

I purchased the stock initially for the following reasons:

- Defensive play in an uncertain market outlook.
- Low relative P/E considering the earnings projections 85/86 which I considered conservative if you would account for a substantial drop in the U.S. dollars.
- Good yield—therefore limiting the downside risk in a low interest environment.
- Resistant in an uncertain economic environment; possible stagnation and/or deflation.
- Further most likely share repurchase programs (which would be even more attractive if my assumption of future lower interest rates would be true).

I purchased an initial position of approx. 100,000 shs. between $59 and $60. When the stock moved up steadily and the volume increased, I decided to average up. I bought another 50,000 shs. between $61 and $64.625, approx. half my initial position because at the $64 level the downside on the stock was greater and not to bring my average cost of the total position too far up. Rumors of a possible take-over was not the reason I purchased the stock initially, but encouraged me to increase my position at higher prices.

> *SEC:* "You indicated that *Mr. X advised you that you could go into the SEC and in effect tell a false story and that the SEC would not be able to do anything about it.* Did he indicate to you a basis for why he thought that was a likely result?"
>
> *Pletscher:* "Yes. Mr. X told us that he has experience with the SEC and he and people that he knows have been called to the SEC for testimonies. Mr. X then said, *'You just tell the SEC what you want to tell them,'* and *he and other people went there before, just lied to the SEC and walked out there without any problem since the SEC does not have any proof.* He then said that in this particular case the SEC could also not identify a pattern, and if we would confirm to the SEC that we made the investment decisions and . . . bought these shares for managed portfolios, *this would be the end of the story.*"

Levine's plan, then, was threefold. To create the appearance that the suspicious accounts were managed by the bank, to provide the bankers with investment rationale for buying the suspicious stocks and to feed the lies to attorney Harvey Pitt. Levine believed that because he was a former SEC general counsel, Pitt's credibility at the agency would extend to his clients. Everyone would accept the story and the trail would dead-end at Fried, Frank's Washington office.

But the tale would have a different ending. To have any chance of success, Levine's cover-up required the ironclad support of his Bank Leu cohorts. To a man, they would have to stick to the story about managed accounts and hold up the shields of

Swiss and Bahamian secrecy laws to protect Levine's identity.

That show of solidarity started coming apart at the seams when Pletscher—always a nervous participant in the scheme—began fearing the SEC would see through the ruse. This turned to panic when Meier, also sensing trouble, resigned from the bank in mid-December 1985. Soon after, Bank Leu asked Harvey Pitt to negotiate a deal with the SEC.

In what SEC attorney John Sturc calls "a delicious irony," the lawyer Levine had recommended wound up tying the noose around his neck. In the agreement Pitt worked out with the SEC, the bank agreed to testify about the Levine account, coming clean on its code names, modus operandi, stock trades and cash balances. In return, Bank Leu would be granted immunity from prosecution.

Although Levine's name was initially withheld because Bank Leu feared that revealing his identity would break Bahamian secrecy law, a high-level showdown among the SEC, Bank Leu, Fried, Frank and Bahamian attorney general Paul Adderly broke that deadlock. Bowing to pressure from the United States, the Bahamian government authorized Bank Leu to pierce the veil of secrecy, revealing Mr. X's true identity.

Within days, Dennis Levine was finished. Booked, handcuffed and led away for a night in jail, he would soon be pleading guilty to two counts of tax evasion, one count of securities fraud and one count of perjury. In an effort to reduce his ultimate sentence, he would also be turning into one of the most prolific informants in SEC history. During the following months, Levine would unwind the details of his trading scheme, naming names, citing figures and exposing the accomplices he'd spun into his web, leading ultimately to the biggest catch of all—Ivan Boesky.

Although the SEC is officially mum on how it nailed Boesky, sources close to the investigation give the following account.

Suspicious of Boesky's perfect timing in a string of takeover-related investments, the SEC had monitored his transactions for years, finding a questionable pattern of trades but no evidence that he benefited from inside information. Without such evidence as the handwritten notes found in the Chinese-food containers that broke open the Skadden Arps case, Boesky could simply claim that his success was based on thorough research and an enviable instinct for the market.

"I had no doubt that Boesky was trading on whispers from one or several inside sources and neither did the SEC," says a prominent arb whose joy at Boesky's arrest was thinly concealed. "He'd take these gigantic positions on transactions where the spread was just too small to justify unless you had some way of knowing that there was no risk at all. And because Boesky was never reckless or stupid, everyone knew he had to be getting guaranteed information.

"But the government couldn't go on that alone. The SEC's strategy for going after inside traders is to build so strong a case against them before they're indicted that two things will happen. First, they'll settle without a trial, and second, and more important, they'll rat on others in order to save themselves. Confronted with overwhelming evidence—and with the jail sentence that could lead to—even the tough nuts like Ivan turn to jelly and tell what they know about their accomplices. This is Gary Lynch's MO and it's been extremely effective. With each arrest, he gets deeper and deeper into the vortex of insider trading."

The airtight case against Boesky started to take shape when Dennis Levine, faced with "overwhelming evidence," recognized that the only way to reduce his own jail sentence was to cooperate with Lynch and his colleagues. He started by revealing the identity of his peer accomplices including Robert Wilkis, Ira Sokolow, Ilan Reich and David Brown. Still hoping to collect on the $2.4 million Boesky owed him, Levine (who would need the money dearly after losing both his Drexel job and his Bank Leu nest egg) failed at first to incriminate the arb.

"Every time the SEC asked Dennis about Ivan, he'd say, 'Oh, Ivan's a straight guy. He's clean,'" one source comments. "Dissatisfied with this, the government lawyers, who were now drilling the other minor players in Levine's ring, asked Wilkis who else Dennis was involved with. Immediately, Wilkis fingered

Boesky. Although Ivan and Dennis had made a pact to keep their arrangement under wraps, it seems that Dennis was so proud to be working with Boesky that he couldn't contain himself. On several occasions he'd bragged to Wilkis about his relationship with Boesky and now Wilkis was telling it to the SEC."

Confronted with Wilkis's testimony and with telephone records linking him to the arb, Levine finally admitted Boesky's complicity and, in an effort to save his own skin—job offer and hero worship notwithstanding—agreed to tape-record conversations with Boesky. In one call reportedly staged for this purpose, Levine is said to have pressed Boesky for the fee owed him and was told that the money would be paid.

Armed with Boesky's trading records and with the testimony of his inside source, the SEC moved in on Ivan the Terrible in the early fall of 1986, about six months after Levine was arrested and more than a month before the charges against the arbitrager were publicly announced. That the government would be coming after him was no surprise to Boesky, who had suffered through a succession of sleepless nights ever since the SEC revealed that Levine was nabbed and was singing in order to save himself. In August, Boesky had even announced to his fellow directors of the Beverly Hills Hotel Corporation that he was under investigation. But from all indications, he believed, as did his cohort Levine until the very end, that he could beat the system and get away with it, that the government could not build a case strong enough to convict him.

"But that fantasy apparently ended when Ivan got a look at what the SEC really had on him," says a lawyer familiar with the case. "It was at that point that he recognized he was caught in a trap he just couldn't wiggle out of. That's when he called Pitt [Harvey Pitt, the same lawyer who represented Bank Leu] and asked him what to do. The way I see it, Pitt must have told him to do the only sane thing: admit his guilt in exchange for lenient treatment from the government. In other words, strike the best bargain he could get."

Which is precisely what he did. But to many, the deal Boesky struck with the government was tipped in his favor. He settled with the SEC without admitting or denying guilt and in criminal proceedings with the U.S. Attorney's Office admitted to a single count of securities fraud, carrying a maximum jail sentence of five years—far less than Dennis Levine's potential twenty-year confinement. Whether Boesky will ever serve time is a subject of much debate on Wall Street. Some believe that his cooperation with the government will buy his freedom; others insist that for the government, including the judiciary, to send out a clear signal against insider trading, the biggest trader of all will have to spend at least a year behind bars.

What's more, the settlement left Boesky a rich man, free to conduct the ultimate inside trade of his career. Although his settlement required the payment of $100 million to the government ($50 million as a return of his illegal profit and a $50 million penalty), he was left with enormous assets including his wife's majority ownership of the Beverly Hills Hotel (a property worth more than $100 million), a palatial estate in Chappaqua, New York (complete with lanes named "Wall" and "Broad," a Manhattan co-op and assorted bank accounts and personal investments. In short, he was allowed to keep enough money to retain his status as one of the wealthiest men in America.

As if that were not generous enough, the SEC also allowed him to sell off $440 million of his fund's stock holdings before news of his settlement reached the public. Knowing full well that the market would nosedive once the terms that required Boesky to sever his investment activities by April 1988 were revealed, Boesky sought permission to liquidate a substantial portion of his firm's portfolio while stock prices were relatively high. The SEC agreed to this, ostensibly to protect the market from wholesale chaos and from the possibility of an even more drastic drop in prices if it became known that Boesky was liquidating. But the SEC authorized what many others on the Street saw as the granddaddy of inside trades. On November 14, 1986, the SEC revealed Boesky's complicity in what had already emerged, through Levine's arrest earlier in the year, as the greatest insider trading scheme in Wall Street history. Days after the Boesky announcement, prices on many of the issues he sold plunged by as much as 15 percent, causing the rest of the arbitrage community to suffer losses of up to $1 billion. In contrast, Boesky's savings from trading before the market decline may have totaled $100 million—the same amount as his settlement with the SEC.

As the head of stock trading at a large Wall Street firm was quoted: "It's the irony of ironies. The biggest inside information is that Boesky is being put out of business, and he gets to trade on it first."*

While it appears that Boesky walked away a winner in his confrontation with the government, the price paid to win his cooperation may prove, ultimately, to be a bargain.

"The SEC's real objective goes beyond the prosecution of a string of inside traders," says one source who has seen the government's case develop first hand. "The ultimate goal is to get to the triad of investment bankers, arbitragers and corporate raiders who have been passing inside information between one another and using it to manipulate the market. Getting Boesky was important in itself but not as important as using him to get at the real root of the problem."

Boesky's deal with the government required him to lead the feds to other inside traders caught up in his web of market manipulations. One of the first to be implicated was the man many rated as the best investment banker on the Street—Martin A. Siegel, co-head of Drexel Burnham's M&A machine.

A Wall Street wunderkind, Siegel had become a legend in 1982 when he engineered a successful PacMan defense for his client Martin Marietta Corp., which turned the tables on its prospective acquirer, the Bendix Corp., by launching a counter takeover. Siegel had gained fame and affluence before his thirty-third birthday, but in a familiar pattern on Wall Street, it wasn't enough. Finding his lifestyle escalating faster than his earnings,

*George Anders, "Boesky Fund Sold Big Blocks of Securities," *The Wall Street Journal*, November 20, 1986, p. 3.

Siegel—who then worked at the patrician and somewhat dowdy investment bank of Kidder, Peabody—allegedly cut a deal with Boesky similar to Dennis Levine's, whereby he would pass information to the arb, claiming a percentage of Boesky's profits in return.

The scheme began in earnest with the Bendix–Martin Marietta confrontation, with Siegel tipping Boesky to his client's imminent bid for Bendix, and continued through 1984. Siegel would alert Boesky to inside information gleaned from his role as a Kidder investment banker, and at the end of each year, the two men would meet to settle their secret account. Boesky would report how much he'd made and how much he owed Siegel, and later have a courier deliver Siegel's booty in a suitcase. By the time Siegel threw cold water on the relationship—after learning to his horror that Boesky was the subject of a continuing SEC investigation—he'd collected about $700,000. Boesky reportedly earned $33 million on the information Siegel fed to him.

Although Siegel never formally told Boesky that he wanted out, he stopped wiring the arb into Kidder's deals, hoping in this way to limit his exposure should Ivan fall victim to a government dragnet. But it was too late. Once Boesky was nabbed and agreed to cooperate with the authorities to save his own hide, he pointed immediately to Siegel, knowing that his help in the capture of so prominent an investment banker would play well before a judge.

For Siegel, the end was near. Two days before Boesky's indictment was announced, the investment banker, by then a senior Drexel executive, was meeting with Marty Lipton when federal agents burst into the lawyer's office, slapping Siegel with a subpoena. Recognizing that the government had a strong case against him and that a protracted legal fight would only lead to more severe penalties, Siegel pleaded guilty to two felony counts and agreed to cooperate with the continuing investigation.

Four months later, the results of that cooperation would hit the financial community like the fallout from a 50 megaton bomb. On February 12, 1987, a platoon of federal agents barged into the office of Richard Wigton, Kidder Peabody's chief arbitrager—a man thought to be as close to a Boy Scout as anyone on Wall

Street. Frisked and handcuffed, Wigton was led away in full view of the firm's stunned employees. Within moments, the same shocking scene repeated itself at Goldman Sachs, where top arbitrager Robert Freeman was arrested in his 24th-floor office. Earlier, Timothy Tabor, a nomad arb who had served stints at Kidder, Merrill Lynch and Chemical Bank, was nabbed in his apartment.

Cited for violations of the securities laws, the three men were fingered by an informant initially identified by the government as CS-1 (confidential source 1). But the source turned out to be none other than Marty Siegel. According to the government, the men were involved in an intricate trading scheme in which Siegel, while working at Kidder in both the arbitrage and M&A departments, leaked client information to his arb colleagues Wigton and Tabor and to Goldman Sachs's Freeman, who allegedly returned the favor, providing Kidder with inside information on Goldman clients. Wigton, Tabor and Freeman deny the government's charges.

When Wall Street had time to react to the latest bombshell and to contemplate the fall of one of its towering figures, Marty Siegel, the response was one of shock and bewilderment.

"If Wigton and Tabor were involved, that you could understand," says an investment banker who worked with Siegel. "Marty was a colossal salesman. He could convince people to do things that under any other circumstances they wouldn't even consider. If these guys are guilty as charged, they were probably Siegel's tools—doing what he told them to do.

"But that still leaves the question of how Marty could have gotten involved in insider trading. It's a question I keep asking myself over and over again. You're talking about a man who was the world's best investment banker. One with that rare combination of rocket-scientist smarts and a Hollywood personality. He could structure a deal where, by all rational standards, there wasn't anything to structure and then could turn around and sell it to everyone who, before he started pitching it, didn't want it to happen. The man could make miracles happen.

"That he would get involved in an illicit arrangement with Boesky—and that he'd do it for $700,000—is shocking. Unbelievable. In his world, $700,000 just didn't mean all that much. The only way I can understand it is that he thought he would get more from Boesky, and Boesky just screwed him. In the game they were playing, you can't appeal your payoff to a higher authority. Or, he believed there was no chance, not even a remote possibility, that he'd get caught. If he thought that, it was the first big mistake of his career. The one that ended it.

"Now word is out that with Boesky and Siegel turned stoolies, a shocking number of prominent people are going to be implicated as insider traders. Legal legends, heads of investment banks—we're talking household names here."

In one line of investigation, the SEC is looking into a disturbing pattern between Boesky and Drexel Burnham. Close study of Boesky's trading activities has turned up an uncanny track record of his buying stocks just prior to a positive announcement by Drexel clients. In more than a dozen such investments, Levine was not Boesky's source.

For example, Boesky began buying the shares of Pacific Lumber in September 1986. Three days later, Drexel's client, the Maxxam Group, announced a plan to tender for Pacific Lumber's stock. (Maxxam's decision to go after Pacific Lumber was allegedly based on recommendations from Drexel's Beverly Hills office.)

In another deal—one in which Drexel executives were involved as principals—AM International, a troubled office-equipment manufacturer, considered making a bid for Harris Graphics, a printing-machine maker that Drexel had taken private in 1983. When the company went private, a number of Drexel officers became Harris stockholders and one served on its board of directors.

In the summer of 1985, the Drexel people—eager to engineer a sale of Harris in order to claim substantial gains on their stock—touted a deal with AM International and even hosted a meeting between the two companies at Drexel's Los Angeles outpost. Boesky, who already owned some Harris shares, soon began increasing his accumulation in the stock, claiming 8.4 percent of the outstanding shares by October 1985. Although the talks seesawed on and off for some time, AM International wound up making an offer for the company.

While complicity on the part of Drexel (which is itself the subject of investigations by the SEC and a federal grand jury) or its executives has not been proven, the pattern of Boesky's buys so close on the heels of the firm's transactions might lead to suspicions that the arb may have had more than one source at the investment bank. If one considers Drexel's pervasive influence over the M&A business, it would be the ideal source for the man who described arbitrage as Wall Street's "best-kept money-making secret," but who had another little secret of his own.

Related to the Drexel line of inquiry is the SEC's investigation into a possible conspiracy among arbitragers, investment bankers and corporate raiders.

"The government is out to prove—and may well do so—that the arbs were principal players in a scheme to put companies into play and thus to manipulate the market," says a securities lawyer with close contacts in the government. "They see it this way: An arb and a raider—joined together by an investment bank that serves them both—identify a company that, because of its poor stock performance or hidden assets, would be ideal for a takeover attempt. Together they start accumulating shares in the company, keeping their holdings below the five-percent stake that requires notification [to] the SEC. Then, when they approach that level, they have the banker spread a rumor that the target company is in play. When investors (including other arbs) seeking a takeover play jump into the stock, causing its price to rise, the manipulators bail out with a handsome profit.

"The beauty of teamwork. The SEC is convinced this goes on. With Boesky's help, they're trying to prove it."

With Boesky actively cooperating with the SEC's continuing investigation, all observers close to the probe agree that it is only a

NINE TRANSACTIONS IN THE BOESKY INVESTIGATION

Transaction	Boesky's purchases	News announcement	Drexel role	Remarks
Victor Posner acquires control of Fischbach	Boesky purchases Fishbach shares beginning April 1984	Posner to seek control of Fischbach, announced July 1984	Drexel finances Posner	First Executive, led by Fred Carr, a Drexel client, also acquires large Fischbach stake
AM International acquires Harris Graphics	Boesky increases Harris stake August 1985, at time of Harris secret talks with AM	AM bids for Harris April 1986	Drexel officials are major Harris shareholders; Drexel initiates talks between AM and Harris	A Reliance company, led by Saul Steinberg, a Drexel client, increases Harris stake beginning March, as secret talks with AM resume
Lorimar merges with Telepictures, then acquires assets from MGM/UA Entertainment	Boesky holds large stake in Lorimar prior to merger with Telepictures to form Lorimar-Telepictures and MGM/UA prior to its acquisition by Ted Turner. United Artists stock also involved	Boesky purchases follow initial news reports; precede numerous developments as aspects of the transactions are revised and refinanced and stocks fluctuate accordingly	Lorimar, Lorimar-Telepictures and MGM/UA Entertainment are all Drexel clients; Drexel officials were involved in the series of transactions	

Transaction	Boesky's purchases	News announcement	Drexel role	Remarks
Occidental Petroleum negotiates to acquire Diamond Shamrock	Boesky acquires stake in Diamond Shamrock prior to January 1985 talks	Occidental and Diamond announce possible merger January 1985; talks break down soon after	Drexel issues fairness opinion for Occidental in negotiations	
Maxxam acquires Pacific Lumber	Boesky begins acquiring large stake in Pacific Lumber September 27, 1985	Maxxam announces bid for Pacific Lumber September 30, 1985	Drexel initiates transaction; represents Maxxam	
Carl Icahn proposes bid for Phillips Petroleum	Boesky acquires large stake prior to Icahn proposal	Icahn announces bid proposal February 1985	Drexel finances Icahn	Boesky urges Icahn to fight for control of Phillips
Trans World repurchases shares amid rumors Golden Nugget will launch bid for Trans World	Boesky acquires Trans World stake amid takeover rumors	Share repurchase announced May 1985; expanded April 1986. Revlon buys Trans World stake and threatens bid October 1986	Drexel represents Golden Nugget; no bid materializes. Later, Drexer represents Revlon in threatened bid for Trans World	Boesky held conversations with Trans World regarding his stake. Golden Nugget disclosed it held close to 5% of Trans World's stock at end of 1985. Revlon, backed by Drexel,

Mesa Petroleum bids for Unocal	Boesky acquires Unocal stake prior to Mesa bid	Mesa announces bid April 1985	Drexel finances Mesa bid	later threatens bid; Trans World responds with a liquidation plan
Wickes acquires Gulf & Western's consumer products division	Boesky begins accumulating G&W stock before deal announced	Wickes and G&W announce sale June 1985	Drexel initiates deal; finances Wickes	G&W undertakes share repurchase; Boesky held conversations with G&W; Boesky disposed of stake

Source: The Wall Street Journal, December 5, 1986, p. 23. Reprinted by permission of *The Wall Street Journal,* © Dow Jones & Company, Inc. 1986. All rights reserved.

matter of time before other names are swept into the scandal—a chilling prospect for Wall Street; one that has cast a pall over the takeover business and that for the first time in years has diminished the flow of inside information. But the question is: Will it last? Or should it?

To one school of thought, there's nothing wrong with inside trading. Everyone, they say, looks for a tip. Some are just better at it.

"Insider trading really isn't such a bad thing," says Dennis Levine's former Baruch professor Jack Francis. "The newspapers have made Dennis out to be a bad person who made all these millions from this horrendous crime called insider trading. But it's really not such a horrendous crime. . . . Dennis wasn't taking money from orphans and widows. His was a victimless crime.

"What about the market's credibility? Also a non-issue. People who worry about the market's credibility are naive. John Q. Public doesn't give a thought to credibility. He has no plan, no system for investing. He buys stock when he gets a tax refund, hits the lotto or inherits money, and he sells it when he needs money for a vacation or for a down payment on a house. And how does he choose his stocks? From tips he gets from his broker. Tips he thinks are hot but are about as useful as yesterday's weather report.

"John Q. Public wants inside information. His only bitch is that what he gets isn't as good—not by a country mile—as the real stuff."

While there is much truth to this, the real issue is not whether inside trading is evil, but whether it has a disruptive impact on the capital markets. And here, the answer must be yes. If the stock exchanges become rigged in favor of a ring of insiders, more than a few arbs or institutions will suffer. Not only will the nation and the capitalist system on which it is based be tainted— a sorry reflection on the country—but the functioning of the free market itself is threatened.

This much said, has inside trading been dealt a fatal blow? Will the fraternity of insiders resist the temptation to reap windfall profits once the heat of the Levine–Boesky case passes, once

SEC ramrod Gary Lynch moves into higher office? Sadly enough, the prognosis is not good. In all likelihood, inside trading—long a dark force in the stock exchanges—will resume, perhaps stronger than ever as the securities markets grow more complex, more multinational.

Ike Sorkin, the former SEC regional director who supervised the Yuppie Five case before returning to private law practice, is proud of his accomplishments but at the same time realistic about the chances of snaring cagey insiders who conceal their trading through a multinational prism. In what he calls his "hypothetical horror scenario," Sorkin foresees a convoluted scheme that would take, by all accounts, something short of a miracle to crack.

"It is three A.M. New York time. The stock of United States–based ABC Corporation, listed on the Tokyo exchange, suddenly starts rising, slowly at first but then like a Delta rocket. The next day, XYZ Company announces that it has made a deal to acquire ABC for $1 billion. Because the stock ran up before the announcement—a good indication of insider trading—the SEC is called in to investigate.

"What does it find? A multinational nightmare: the ABC purchases were made by a Hong Kong bank acting for a Lichtenstein trust. The trustee—a Belgian with dual citizenship in Belgium and Lichtenstein—is placing his orders for three Panamanians living in Nigeria.

"How long will it take to find out who's really behind the trading? Hong Kong, Lichtenstein and Belgium have strict secrecy laws and God only knows about Nigeria. Even if the SEC learns the identity of the traders, what does it have? Mr. Wong at the Hong Kong bank knows only that he speaks to Mr. Von Stupp at the Lichtenstein trust. Von Stupp, in turn, simply takes his orders from a Panamanian trust, the trustee of which is a Venezuelan who takes his orders from a Canadian citizen living in Nigeria. The Canadian is a cousin by marriage of one of the investment bankers in New York working on the ABC deal. That individual leaked the information to Nigeria using code names and pay telephones.

"After the SEC gets through the secrecy laws in the various

countries and ultimately locates the Canadian, he comes in and takes the Fifth. Because there's no connection on paper between the investment banker and the Canadian, there's still a lot of investigating to do before you have a case. Maybe they'll be able to make the connections and maybe they won't. It's a nightmare. You can spend years looking into it and come away with nothing to show for your efforts."

More than this foreign intrigue, however, the real problem is in Wall Street's lack of concern with insider trading, and lack of meaningful controls to prevent it. The truth is that the lawyers, investment bankers, proxy solicitors, PR men, printers and confidants are too preoccupied with making money to be concerned with ethics or fair play in the markets on which they base their livelihoods.

Yes, the word on the Street may be "mum" now, but once the current crop of investigations have petered out, leaks, gossip, cross-pollination, run-ups and anomalies are bound to take over again. Even an SEC attorney admits that the victory may be short-lived.

"The only way to stop the inside traders permanently is to keep a fire at their feet, but that may be impossible."

Perhaps a prominent arbitrager sums it up best: "Wall Street's afraid now. But Wall Street has a short memory."